Reaffirming

REAFFIRMING THE CHURCH OF ENGLAND

Why it is, what it is and how it is

HUGH MONTEFIORE

First published 1995
Triangle
SPCK
Holy Trinity Church
Marylebone Road
London NW1 4DU

British Library Cataloguing-in-Publication Data
A catalogue record of this book is available from the British Library

ISBN 0-281-04841-X

Typeset by David Gregson Associates, Beccles, Suffolk
Printed in Great Britain by BPC Paperbacks Ltd

Contents

Contents

Preface

The Church of England has recently taken a drubbing from those who do not like it or who know little about it. Journalists who never darken the church porch have been happy to generalise about congregations they have never seen. Disaffected members have been quick to spread abroad the idea that the Church of England is in disarray. Some Roman Catholic writers, rather surprisingly, have been quick to seize the opportunity of running down the Church of England.

As a result many ordinary members of a local parish church do not know quite where they stand. What is more, they do not know where the Church of England stands. It is inevitable that they should suffer some loss of confidence. The same is true of those who are on the fringe of the Church, the occasional worshippers and those who have in the past been well-wishers.

What are the real facts about the Church of England? This short book attempts to set them out. What does the Church of England stand for? I have tried to explain. I have made no attempt to whitewash the Church of England. Like all other institutional churches, it has done some things in the past of which it should be ashamed. But it also has done other things of which it can rightly be very proud. It does not pretend to be perfect. It does not pretend to be better than any other church. But its record shows it to be a church which is seeking to be faithful and obedient to the Christian gospel.

The book has been designed with many short chapters so that you can either read it as a whole, or use it as a work of reference to look up a particular point.

My thanks yet again to Dr David Edwards, who has of his kindness read through my manuscript and made some helpful suggestions. For any shortcomings I am of course solely responsible.

HUGH MONTEFIORE

The Church in England up to the Reformation

Many people seem to think that the Church of England was founded by King Henry VIII. In fact what he did was to begin its reformation. The Church in England began over a thousand years before that. It started as part of the Western Church under the control of the Pope in Rome. It continued as such until the Reformation, when a process began which denied the authority of the Pope, so that the Church in England became known (in contradistinction to the Roman Catholic Church) as the Church of England. I have to start with some potted history to explain this. Sorry!

THE CELTIC CHURCH

The story that St Joseph of Arimathea (who assisted at Jesus's burial) landed in Britain and went to Glastonbury is only a legend. No one quite knows when Christianity first appeared in Britain during the Roman imperial occupation of the country. Alban was our first known martyr, killed about AD 308. We know there were Christians in England a century before that, because they were mentioned by the early Christian writers Tertullian and Origen in the second century AD. When the Romans withdrew in the fifth century and Britain was overrun by pagan invaders, Christians were forced to retreat to Wales, and England became again a heathen country.

THE CONVERSION OF ENGLAND

In 597 Augustine landed in Kent on orders from Pope Gregory the Great and soon afterwards baptised King Ethelbert at Canterbury. The story goes that Gregory's interest was whetted when he saw some slaves from England and exclaimed 'Non Angli sed angeli' (not English but angels). The mission in England prospered. Augustine became the first Archbishop of Canterbury, and the present primate, Dr George Carey, is the 104th archbishop in direct descent from him. Anglicans deny that there was discontinuity at the Reformation. So much for the myth that the Church of England began in the reign of King Henry VIII!

Of course Augustine's mission did not convert the whole country. Christianity in the North was planted through the work of Aidan, who came from the Scottish island of Iona. There was some trouble integrating the traditions of the old Celtic Church and the more recent Roman mission, but this was achieved at the Synod of Whitby in 633. One who played a key part in this reconciliation was Cuthbert, whose bones are now in a shrine in Durham Cathedral.

THE REFORMATION IN EUROPE

There was real piety in the medieval Church in England, intermingled with superstition. Monasteries and nunneries abounded, and they had collected very considerable wealth. However, by the sixteenth century the Church in Europe as a whole had fallen into decay with many abuses. The Reformation that ensued involved in many European countries setting up Protestant churches over against the Roman Catholic Church, despite the fact that the Lutherans wanted to reform the Roman Catholic Church, not overthrow it. In England and Wales, however, the Reformation took a different form. There was no great spiritual leader like Luther in Germany or Calvin in Switzerland. It began not as the result of a popular demand for reform, but with an act of State. But by the end of the reign of Elizabeth I, England had become definitely, even fanatically, Protestant – partly patriotic but partly Puritan.

THE REFORMS OF HENRY VIII

In the swirling European politics of the sixteenth century, dynastic marriages were very important. Henry VIII badly needed a male heir. His wife, Catherine of Aragon, bore him Mary (later Queen of England) but no live male child. Henry began his reign as a devout Catholic, and was given the title 'Defender of the Faith' by the Pope for a book of which he was co-author, taking issue with Luther on the sacraments. Catherine of Aragon had originally been married to his elder brother who died before this marriage was even consummated and never came to the throne. After he had married Catherine, Henry began to think that God was denying him a male heir because he should not have married his deceased brother's wife, despite the Pope's dispensation. He determined to have the marriage annulled, for which there was good precedent. The Pope, squeezed by international politics, had to refuse. Thereupon Henry decided to take the law into his own hands and appointed Thomas Cranmer as Archbishop of Canterbury. By this time he had distanced himself from Catherine, and had made Anne Boleyn (whom he subsequently married) pregnant. Cranmer, who believed in the 'divine right of kings', annulled his marriage with Catherine, and married him and Anne.

THE BREAK WITH ROME

Recent research has shown that the people of England were deeply religious, devoted to their old traditions. Although the English church had in the past been granted some liberties by the Pope, there was no great demand in England for change in the church. John Wyclif (1329–84) had said that the Pope's claims were ill founded in Scripture; he questioned orthodox theories about the Holy Communion; and he wanted the Scriptures read in English. His teaching was continued by the Lollards until the middle of the fifteenth century. But Wyclif, although he was English, had more influence on the Reformation in Bohemia than in England.

Henry originally had no intention of doing away with Catholic traditions. He was concerned only to break away entirely from the jurisdiction of Rome, not for theological reasons but so that he could remarry and have a male heir. He dominated Parliament, which passed a number of measures to bring about this total break. He even declared himself 'supreme head' of the Church of England. He caused a copy of the English Bible to be set up in every parish church. For the first time the common people, if they could read, could find out for themselves the contents of the Bible. As Henry grew older, his religion became more reactionary, as is exemplified in his Six Articles Act. His character, which in his early years had been so promising (he was athletic, musical, intelligent and theologically literate) gravely deteriorated in middle age. He needed money and dissolved the monasteries, using most of their wealth to reward his supporters or to finance warfare; and, as is well known, he demanded annulments of his various other marriages with the result that he was married six times.

The way in which the Church of England broke with Rome is not very edifying. But it must be remembered that in those days democracy as we know it had not yet evolved. The monarch was supreme, and was generally regarded as having a divine right to rule. Religion played such a central part in the life of a nation that decisions about the Church were made not by the people but from the top downwards. As we shall see, sin certainly entered into the way the English Reformation took place. If the Pope had not had his hand forced by international pressure, it might conceivably not have happened. But it did happen, and there were many deeper currents affecting the turn of events; medieval Catholicism was breaking up, the unity of Christendom was being replaced by nationalism, and the new learning was making people ask questions where before tradition had simply been taken for granted. Spiritual renewal came in Protestant lands through the rediscovery of the Bible, and in Latin lands through the Counter-Reformation. In England it took a unique form; and despite all the factors involving the King's sex life and his desire for a male heir, Anglicans like to think that God's providential hand can be seen behind it.

2

The Reformation Settlement

The Reformation Settlement in England did not, thank goodness, involve the fighting of a religious war. But the times were very unsettled, and there was real suffering and even bloodshed on both sides, Protestant and Catholic.

The Church of England was not a new church which began at the Reformation, like some other churches. In that sense it is not a Protestant church. But it is a church which protests against what it sees as the errors of Rome, and in that sense it *is* a Protestant church.

Fortunately the distance between the Church of England and the Roman Catholic Church is not now as great as it once was. The Anglican–Roman Catholic International Commission (ARCIC), which was set up after Archbishop Michael Ramsey's visit to the Pope in 1970, has produced a series of reports which show what seems to be an almost miraculous convergence on many points of belief, and these give great hope for the future. At the same time some stubborn points of difference still remain concerning Christian belief (for example, the Roman Catholic doctrines about Mary, that the Mother of Jesus was born without original sin and that at her death she was physically taken up into heaven). There are also differences on moral matters (for example, the Roman Catholic veto on any form of artificial contraception) as well as over jurisdiction (Anglicans reject the Pope's claim to 'immediate jurisdiction' over the whole Church). Although the Anglican and Roman Catholic Churches agree far more than they differ with each other, there are still important differences to be overcome.

At the 'Glorious Revolution' when William and Mary acceded to the throne after the departure of the Roman Catholic James II in 1688, Parliament determined never again to repeat this experience, so it imposed the Accession Declaration and the Coronation Oath, in which the sovereign has to swear to uphold the Protestant religion as established by law. These requirements have already been modified, and there is pressure for them to be further amended. The word 'Protestant' in these declarations reflects the situation at the time when they were first introduced; but it is not yet wholly irrelevant today.

As we have seen, the original split with Rome under Henry VIII did not come about for theological reasons. But Anglicans believe that the providence of God was at work liberating them from what they regard as the errors of Rome. To understand how the reformed Church of England still remained Catholic despite this breach with the mainstream Church of the West we shall have to consider the way in which its reformation came about.

THE REIGN OF EDWARD VI

Henry VIII was succeeded by his young and sickly son Edward in 1547. He was only nine years old, so Henry ensured that the boy's uncle would head the Council which ruled the land. He was a reformer, and reformers, some of whom had arrived from overseas, had the upper hand. A lot of furnishings and other objects such as images and censers began to be cleared out of parish churches; and the Communion Table was set up in the chancel or the nave for a celebration of the Lord's Supper rather than as an altar of sacrifice. Within a short time Cranmer had introduced the first English prayer book (considered by some to be his finest work) and its use was enforced by law; three years later in 1552, he produced his second prayer book, which is substantially the same as our present Book of Common Prayer. Cranmer also drew up a series of Articles, placing the Church of England midway between medieval Catholicism and out-and-out reformers. This *via media* ('middle way') was to be an enduring characteristic of the reformed Church of England.

BACK TO ROME UNDER QUEEN MARY

When Edward died at the age of 16, his half-sister Mary succeeded him. Brought up as a strict Catholic by her mother Catherine of Aragon, she brought about the reconciliation of the Church of England with Rome. The Latin Mass was reinstated, together with all the apparatus of Catholic worship. Clergy who under the new regime had been allowed to marry were deprived of their livings if they had done so. Mary's marriage to King Philip of Spain was deeply unpopular in the country, and she was unable to bear him a living child. Embittered and disappointed, Mary became a religious fanatic, convincing herself that God's anger against her and against England could only be appeased by Protestant sacrifice. During the four years of her reign (1554–58) she had 288 martyrs burnt for heresy. (This may be compared with 118 Roman

Catholics put to death for high treason between
1577 and 1603 during the reign of Elizabeth I. Both
figures rightly fill us with revulsion today, but they
must be understood within the context of those
times.)

THE ELIZABETHAN SETTLEMENT

If the Church veered towards Protestantism during
the reign of Edward VI, and then returned to
Roman Catholicism during the reign of Queen
Mary, Queen Elizabeth made a religious settlement
which may have seemed Protestant at the time, but
which in fact – as later became apparent – embodied
the middle way and which produced a lasting settlement. She revived legislation which freed the
Church of England from papal jurisdiction, and
cleared out of parish churches the furnishings,
images and the apparatus of Catholic worship which
Mary had reinstated. (Congregations dislike change,
and these did not all disappear overnight.) At the
same time she determined to keep the church free
of Protestant extremists. Refusing the title of
'supreme head', she called herself 'supreme governor' of the Church. She caused the Prayer Book of
1552 to be revised with the removal of its more
objectionable Protestant features. This was agreed
by Parliament despite the opposition of all the
(Marian) bishops, who naturally wanted to use the
Roman Mass. Two hundred clergy were deprived of
their livings for refusing to use the new book. A fine
was imposed for non-attendance at divine worship.
The reduced number of clergy necessitated a lay
order of ministry to help at non-eucharistic services.
Great care was taken to preserve the continuity of

Anglican orders with the outward sign of the apostolic succession (see further page 59). A revision of ecclesiastical law was begun but abandoned; instead Elizabeth had new canons added to the old ones, although she did not formally give them her Royal Assent. Matthew Parker, whom the Queen had appointed Archbishop of Canterbury, brought order out of chaos. He ruled with mildness and moderation, protecting both Marian bishops and Protestant extremists, and ensuring a Catholic spirit in the reformed Church of England. His Thirty-Nine Articles of Religion steered a middle course between the two extremes of the Reformation and Counter-Reformation. Ecclesiastical vestments in use during Edward VI's time were allowed, although the strong Puritan element in the Church preferred a simple church habit.

If there was pressure from the side of Puritanism, the same was also true of Roman Catholicism. Elsewhere in Europe the Jesuits were active in promoting the Roman Counter-Reformation, and this also happened in Britain. Unfortunately the Pope published a bull declaring Elizabeth illegitimate and calling on Roman Catholics to secure her deposition. This had the effect of making all Roman Catholics regarded as potential traitors to the State. Legislation was passed depriving them not only of religious liberty but also of many other human rights and even of life. England at that time was something of a police state with torture, informers and double agents to keep Elizabeth I safely on the throne and so to keep the Church of England safe too. The defeat of the Spanish Armada put paid to Roman Catholics' immediate hopes of regaining Britain for Roman Catholicism.

It was during the time of Elizabeth that there began to grow up a distinctive Anglican theology. The two most famous of its theologians were John Jewel, Bishop of Salisbury, who wrote his *Apology for the Anglican Church* and his protegé Richard Hooker, who wrote *The Laws of Ecclesiastical Polity*. These are still Anglican 'classics'. Their emphasis on the three-fold authority of Scripture, tradition and reason laid the foundation for later Anglican theology.

AFTER THE SETTLEMENT

The Church of England emerged from the troubles of the Reformation with a Church which was Catholic in ethos yet reformed and biblical in its liturgy and spirituality. Membership of the Church was made broad in order to incorporate as many people as possible. The idea was to have a church for all English men and women but it failed. Attendance was enforced by law, with the penalty of fines for non-compliance; and troubles still lay ahead over the toleration of Roman Catholics on the one hand, and of non-conformist Protestants on the other. It is important not to romanticise the Settlement. Roman Catholics and Puritans despised it. Bishops had to work at it. It did not really flower until the seventeenth century. Abortive attempts were made to broaden the Church of England, notably by James I at the Hampton Court Conference (which probably failed because of the King's fear of 'No bishop, no king') and at the Restoration by Charles II at the Worcester House talks (which probably failed because the Anglicans were in a position of power; in any case the King became a Roman

Catholic on his deathbed). Different schools of thought within the Church have gained the ascendency at different periods of its subsequent history: the Latitudinarians (Liberals) in the eighteenth century, the Evangelicals after the Evangelical revival at the beginning of the nineteenth century, and the Catholics in the Oxford Movement a little later. Yet the broad outline of the Settlement still remains during the reign of Elizabeth II as it was when it was set up in the reign of Elizabeth I.

This historical background has been necessary to understand the Church of England today. But of course we are concerned here not primarily with the past but with the present. And it is to this that we now turn.

3

The Authority of the Church of England

AUTHORITY

Jesus was once asked 'By what authority are you doing these things?' (and he would not answer (Mark 11. 28–33)). People today ask 'With what authority does the Church of England speak?' Its critics sometimes suggest that because it is an established church, its ultimate authority is the State. This is not the case. The State supports it, 'establishes' it, if you like, but its authority is spiritual in origin. Authority is not an easy word to describe, because it has a wide range of meanings. The *Concise Oxford Dictionary* defines authority thus: 'Power or right to enforce obedience; moral or legal supremacy; the right to command or give an ultimate decision'. It gives another meaning: 'The power to influence the conduct and actions of others; personal or practical influence'.

We must distinguish between the sources from which authority springs, and the structures of authority through which it functions.

SOURCES OF AUTHORITY

The ultimate source of all authority is God. From him there are mediated sources of authority. The Church of England recognises four: Scripture, tradition, reason and experience. We need to look at each of these in turn.

Scripture

First and foremost comes the Bible. It is crucial, because without the Scriptures we would have no knowledge of Jesus Christ when he lived on earth. It is a cardinal belief of Anglicanism that nothing should be received as necessary to salvation except that which can be 'proved by most certain warrants of Holy Scripture'. This is not to say that the Bible contains no errors, or that all its contents are decisive for life today. The Bible is a compendium of many books of different kinds, among them poetry (including love poetry), history, stories, hymns, letters, proverbs, moral maxims and Gospels. Each kind of book has a different main purpose. Again, the Old Testament is the Bible of the Jews (and of course the Bible of Jesus), whereas the New Testament tells us of the events and beliefs of the earliest Christians, including the life, death and resurrection of Jesus Christ. There is, however, a unity to all these books of the Bible in as much as (with the exception of the Book of Esther) they are all about God. Despite differences of interpretation, the Church has recognised the Bible as authoritative for the Christian life, and God has spoken through its pages to very many people.

Tradition

The Holy Spirit who has inspired the authors of the Bible has also guided the Church down the centuries. (This is not to claim that the Church has always followed the guidance of the Spirit, for it has in its history done many terrible things.) This leads us to the second source of authority for Anglicans, the tradition of the Church (of which of course the

Bible itself is part). This tradition is not just a dead inheritance from the past: it is a living reality in the Church today. There must be some kind of development of belief for it has been promised that the Holy Spirit gives us deeper understanding of our faith; and in any case as our culture changes, the truth of one generation has to be 'inculturated' into the language and thought forms of the next. Fresh moral problems arise which did not exist in earlier times. We cannot set aside the wisdom of those who have gone before us and pretend that we are wiser than the Christians of previous centuries. Similarly we cannot accept the tradition of the Church uncritically. We have seen already that the Church of England is not a church that started with the Reformation. We accept much that belonged to earlier tradition, only rejecting that part of it which seems contrary to the fundamentals of scriptural teaching. Tradition (like the Bible) is not infallible, and Anglicans believe that even General Councils of the Church (that is, meetings of bishops who met in early days from all over Christendom) have been mistaken on occasions. 'The doctrine of the Church of England is grounded in the Holy Scriptures and in such teachings of the ancient Fathers and Councils of the Church as are agreeable to the said Scriptures' (Canon A4). This formula did not specify which Fathers or which Councils, but the general meaning is plain: the Church of England was aiming at a reformed Catholicism.

Reason

Bible and tradition are our primary sources of authority, but we cannot just accept everything we find in them uncritically. While we use our minds to understand the Bible and tradition, we use them also to take in new insights and fresh understanding about the world. We must be true to ourselves; and that means that we cannot jettison what we believe to be true just because it seems to be contradicted by the Bible or tradition. For example, we now take evolution for granted in our understanding of how the universe developed, but this knowledge was lacking in earlier centuries. We cannot deny this truth because the first two chapters of Genesis give us a pre-scientific account of creation. What we have to do is to interpret our modern understanding of the world in such a way that the deep religious truths underlying those biblical stories are still retained. There will be some occasions when a fresh understanding of life makes us prefer a modern interpretation to one which we find in the Scriptures. For example, there is a ban on charging interest in the Scriptures, and this was originally endorsed by tradition. But we do not regard it as wicked to earn interest on our capital today. It is one way in which wealth is created. However, we must be very cautious before we overthrow the teaching of Scripture and tradition, and we must always be sure that we retain the religious or moral truths underlying their teaching. For example, the reason underlying the veto on charging interest was the need to protect, in an agricultural economy, those vulnerable people who were most liable to debt. This is relevant today when one thinks of the interest which the developed world is levying on the Third World for its loans.

Experience

Fourthly, we have our own experience to guide us. Take another example. It is unlikely that we would believe in God if we were totally without any experience of his presence (or at least conscious of his real absence). Our feelings are a very important part of our life, and we ignore them at our peril. The 'charismatic' movement in the churches (including the Church of England) has been reminding us of the importance of religious experience. Christianity is not a purely cerebral religion: it is a source of joy and peace as well. But religious feelings are a dangerous guide on their own, so they need to be supplemented by the other sources of authority. One important part of our experience is our moral conscience. Again, our conscience can mislead us, and so we have a duty to see that it is properly 'informed'. All the same we must obey it; and so moral experience becomes a vital part of religious authority.

STRUCTURES OF AUTHORITY

Anglicans believe that authority is not transmitted in one way only, but that it is disseminated in many ways. A report of the 1948 Lambeth Conference (a meeting of the bishops of the Anglican Communion), in a classic description of disseminated authority, put it like this:

> Authority, as inherited by the Anglican Communion from the undivided Church of the early centuries of the Christian era, is single in that it is derived from a single Divine source, and reflects within itself the richness and historicity of the

Divine Revelation, the authority of the eternal Father, the incarnate Son and the life-giving Spirit. It is distributed among Scripture, Tradition, Creeds, the ministry of the Word and Sacraments, the witness of saints and the *consensus fidelium* [that is, the general agreement of practising Christians], which is the continuing experience of the Holy Spirit through His faithful people in the Church. It is a dispersed rather than a centralised authority having many elements which combine, interact with and check each other; these elements together contributing by a process of mutual support, mutual checking and redressing of errors or exaggerations to the many sided fullness of the authority which Christ has committed to his Church.

The resolutions of Anglican bishops who meet every ten years at these Lambeth Conferences are an important element in this structure of authority. However, each national church in the Anglican Communion, although it belongs to the Anglican family, is autonomous. Within the Church of England there is a dual structure of authority; General Synod and diocesan bishops. The former points to the Church of England as an institution, the latter as a divine society. The two structures intermesh, as bishops form one of the three houses of a synod (houses of bishops, priest and laity). Thus the General Synod is an important element of authority but it is not an infallible one. The authority of the house of bishops is another element, as is the authority of the local diocesan bishop within his diocese, particularly when reinforced by synodical approval. These are some of the structures of authority which 'combine, interact with, and check each other'.

REJECTION OF CENTRALISED AUTHORITY

Anglicans reject the centralised or pyramid view of authority in the Church, according to which all authority emanates from the Pope, the Bishop of Rome, who acts collegially with his bishops. There used to be bitter controversy on this, but civilised discussion now takes place. ARCIC has issued two agreed statements on the subject of authority. Although there is now, happily, a large measure of agreement, some major differences still remain.

In the first place, Anglicans cannot find any scriptural ground for the continuing supremacy of the Bishop of Rome. Jesus said to Peter that 'on this rock I will build my church' (Matthew 16.18), and he gave him authority 'to bind and to loose' (probably meaning the power to make moral decisions for the church). Jesus also told him to 'strengthen thy brethren' after his departure (Luke 22.32). But Jesus said nothing whatsoever about the status of Peter's successors as Bishop of Rome. Many Roman Catholics (including those on ARCIC) do not now base their belief in Roman supremacy on the so-called Petrine promises, but for other Roman Catholics these texts still have great influence.

The second reason why Anglicans reject a centralised view of authority in the Church is that the New Testament gives no authority for this. Certainly there were authoritative figures in the primitive church, such as Peter and Paul. Paul tells us that he gave the right hand of fellowship to Peter, James and

John, but this did not stop him on one occasion from opposing Peter to his face, because he was clearly in the wrong (Galatians 2.11).

Thirdly, a centralised authority in the Church may give rise to the imposition on the whole Church of exaggerations and even errors. Even when the Pope does not speak 'infallibly' on matters of faith or morals, his utterances are to be received with 'religious submission'. His claim to universal jurisdiction over the whole Church can also be seen to lead to the imposition on Christians of unwelcome leaders and even unjust decisions. For these reasons the Church of England has a different view of appropriate structures of authority from that of the Roman Catholic Church. These Anglican objections to a centralised authority in the Church do not mean that there is no place for a bishop who holds pre-eminence over the whole Church. As suggested in the ARCIC Report, at some time in the future a much reformed 'Supreme Primate' (presiding bishop) based in Rome could serve as a suitable symbolic figure standing for the whole universal Church.

4

The Doctrine of the Church of England

What does the Church of England believe? I do not mean the beliefs of individual Anglicans, who are likely to differ in the details of their belief, but the basic beliefs of the Church of England as an institution. For example, some churches have their own summary of faith in their 'confession of faith'. The Church of England does not. Its Thirty-Nine Articles of Religion, as we have seen, are a statement of belief made at a particular time which took a middle way between the Catholic and Protestant beliefs of the day. They no longer serve as a contemporary statement of belief, although the Articles are a foundation document which gives the direction of Anglican beliefs, and provides inspiration and guidance for today. In one sense, the Church of England has no faith of its own. This does not mean that it has no faith, but that it holds only the common faith of the one holy catholic and apostolic Church. These common beliefs of the Church are, of course, to be found in the Book of Common Prayer, the ordinal, and the catechism.

BELIEFS OF THE CHURCH AND OF INDIVIDUALS
The beliefs of a church must be distinguished from the beliefs of individual members, because they are not required to hold each and every article of faith in order to be members in good standing of a particular church. The reader need not be alarmed! An

ordinary lay member of the Church of England will not be charged with heresy because of a lack of orthodoxy. It would be surprising, in any church, if every lay person were completely orthodox in belief. What is important is that the church as such should have standards of belief for its members. Naturally special standards are required of those members, such as clergy or Lay Readers, who have been specially authorised to teach the Christian faith.

BAPTISMAL BELIEFS

When a child is to be christened, the parents and godparents are asked several questions, to which they must give a positive answer if the baptism is to proceed. This gives a standard of belief for an ordinary Christian family. In the Alternative Service Book 1980 they are asked whether they turn to Christ, repent of their sins, and renounce evil. They are also asked whether they 'believe and trust in God the Father who made the world, in his Son Jesus Christ who redeemed mankind, and in the Holy Spirit who gives life to the people of God'. The Church of England encourages the baptism of both infants and adults. There is some pressure today to baptise only the children of regular churchgoers, a practice which costs the Church much goodwill and is of doubtful pastoral value. There are also some Anglicans who disapprove of infant baptism altogether. But this ignores constant church practice down the centuries, and also ignores the theology underlying baptism. Baptism marks the initiative of God preceding all our human efforts. It shows the goodwill of God towards all people, and testifies to the solidarity of the family, in which infants take life on trust from their parents. Infant baptism certainly needs to be supplemented by a later occasion when those baptised as infants can publicly make their personal commitment to God in Christ.

CONFIRMATION

These promises at baptism are repeated at confirmation. Children as they grow up should have been helped by parents and others (as well as at Sunday school) to develop as Christians. The Alternative Service Book does not contain the revised catechism, but it exists; and the older one is to be found in the Book of Common Prayer. The catechism was intended to provide what people should know about their faith before they come forward to confirmation. According to the 1662 Prayer Book 'none . . . shall be confirmed, but such as can say the Creed, the Lord's Prayer, and the Ten Commandments; and can also answer to such other Questions as are in the short Catechism contained.' Now that learning by heart is less fashionable, this is no longer required; but all the same the person to be confirmed ought to know their substance.

ORDINATION

Questions are asked of a deacon and of a priest before ordination, and of a bishop before consecration. The questions are the same in each case and have to be answered positively. Some of these questions are about faith and doctrine. Those to be ordained are asked whether they believe that 'the Holy Scriptures contain all things necessary for eternal salvation through faith in Jesus Christ' and whether they 'believe the doctrine of the Christian faith as the Church of England has received it'.

DECLARATION OF ASSENT

A lay person before being admitted to an office in the church, has to make a declaration of assent: so too does a deacon, priest and bishop at ordination or consecration, and also (in the case of a priest) before becoming a vicar or priest-in-charge. They are addressed as follows:

> The Church of England is part of the one, holy, catholic and apostolic Church, worshipping the one true God, Father, Son, and Holy Spirit. It professes the faith uniquely revealed in the Holy Scriptures and set forth in the catholic creeds, which faith the Church is called upon to proclaim afresh in each generation. Led by the Holy Spirit, it has borne witness to Christian truth in its historic formularies, the Thirty-nine Articles of Religion, the Book of Common Prayer, and the Ordering of Bishops, Priests, and Deacons. In the declaration you are about to make, will you affirm your loyalty to this inheritance of faith as your inspiration and guidance under God in bringing the grace and truth of Christ to this generation and making him known to those in your care? (Alternative Service Book 1980)

And the prescribed Declaration is as follows:

> I do so affirm, and accordingly declare my belief in the faith which is revealed in the holy Scriptures and set forth in the catholic creeds and to which the historic formularies of the Church of England bear witness . . . .

This declaration is intentionally very wide. Assent to the Thirty-Nine Articles, which used to be required, and which caused much heart-searching and no little equivocation, is no longer demanded; but they are cited as bearing witness to Christian truth, together with the Prayer Book, as our inspiration and guide in making Christ known today. What is demanded, however, is a declaration of loyalty to the Anglican inheritance of faith as set out above.

THE ANGLICAN INHERITANCE OF FAITH

The Church of England does not lay down in detail just how the Scriptures are to be interpreted or how the catholic creeds are to be understood today; nor does it give a tight compendium of belief because it is a pluralist church which holds within itself a broad spectrum of belief. It is, however, very clear on essentials.

In 1938 a Commission on Christian Doctrine appointed by the Archbishops of Canterbury and York published its report after lengthy debate. It was called *Doctrine in the Church of England* rather than 'the doctrine *of* the Church of England' because it made no claim to define Anglican doctrine. It covers the whole field of Christian belief, and it laid down permissible limits of doctrinal divergence within the Church of England. World War II intervened before the Commission's report could be discussed by the Church. Nonetheless the distinction of its authors, under the chairmanship of William Temple who subsequently became Archbishop of Canterbury, ensures that it contains not merely much wisdom but also a certain inherent authority.

Later reports of a Standing Commission on Christian Doctrine, such as *Christian Believing* (1976) and *Believing in the Church* (1981) continued this discussion; but none of these publications alters the doctrinal requirements laid down in the questions asked during services as outlined above, and in the Declaration of Assent.

GENERAL SYNOD

The General Synod cannot change the doctrine of the Church of England, but it does on occasion have to decide what is in accord with its beliefs. These need to be developed and interpreted so that they are 'inculturated' into contemporary society.

THE BISHOPS

Bishops have a special responsibility for the preservation of the faith; but this does not exclude exploration, and a search to express the unchanging gospel in contemporary language and images.

In 1986 the House of Bishops produced (in response to the ferment caused by the remarks of Dr David Jenkins, then Bishop of Durham) a report on *The Nature of Christian Belief* in which they made it clear that belief in the objective reality of Christ's resurrection and the empty tomb are part of the faith of the Church of England, as is also the belief that Christ is both fully man and fully God, and born of the Virgin Mary. The statement was concerned with the beliefs of the Church of England rather than with the personal convictions of individual bishops. It also made it clear that there is room for both tradition and enquiry in the Church, and that the relation between the two is not simple and never settled. It follows therefore that anyone who questions these beliefs is not being unfaithful to the Church of England, which encourages enquiry and exploration; but such enquiry and exploration does not alter the content of the faith of the Church of England.

RECENT DOCTRINAL LIMITATION

In 1994 a priest who no longer believed in the reality of God, and who held that religion is a purely human creation, had his licence to officiate removed by his diocesan bishop. There is great diversity of belief in the Church of England which is by its nature a pluralist church (see chapter 6). But a priest who holds that God is not real has crossed the boundary of permissible exploration, and such a view is incompatible with the required answers to the questions put to clergy at their ordination. Similarly, to propagate views about the nature of the church which are incompatible with Anglicanism, may rightly be seen as disloyal to the Church of England.

THE ANGLICAN POSITION

Some people have ridiculed the Church of England, alleging that you can believe anything and yet remain a good Anglican. On the contrary, the Church of England's doctrinal position has been rightly described as a very broad channel of belief, but with buoys marked to show the limits on either side beyond which it is dangerous to travel. The universal creeds of Christendom are recited at all major services of Anglican worship, but the Church does not attempt to define too closely mysteries

which are beyond human understanding. The
Church of England permits exploration of belief
within certain limits, and those limits are drawn wide
enough to enable communion within a wide
Christian fellowship.

5

The Worship of the Church of England

FORMAL WORSHIP

Services in the Church of England, unlike most of those used in the Free Churches, are based on written prayers. Although there is room in these services for informal prayers and for silence, the words and structure of the service are laid down in a prayer book. There is always the danger of too much formality, but there are also great advantages. One is that people can follow and participate in the worship in a way which is not always possible when relying only on the impromptu words of the minister. Another is that the worship is properly balanced and does not rely on the preferences of the minister or on his or her favourite themes. Again, members of a congregation can find their way about worship when they visit another church. There is also the feeling that the congregation is not worshipping simply on its own: it is part of the one, holy, catholic and apostolic church, and sharing in a great wave of worship which is worldwide.

The requirement of formal worship does not prevent the holding of informal services in addition. Many churches have Family Services, and some have gatherings and services for open prayer or charismatic worship (including speaking or singing 'in tongues' and the laying on of hands).

THE BOOK OF COMMON PRAYER

Until 1980 the Church of England services were all

taken from the Book of Common Prayer. As we have seen, this was composed by Archbishop Cranmer in a golden age of English prose, and Cranmer himself had a keen ear for language and its natural rhythms.

The principles of the 1662 Prayer Book are well set out in its Preface. It begins: 'It has been the wisdom of the Church of England, ever since the first compiling of her Publick Liturgy, to keep the mean between the two extremes, of too much stiffness in refusing, and of too much easiness in admitting any variation from it.' The Preface goes on to say that changes made from the earlier version of the Prayer Book were for 'the preservation of Peace and Unity in the Church; the procuring of Reverence, and exciting of Piety and Devotion in the publick Worship of God; and the cutting off occasion from them that seek occasion of cavil or quarrel against the Liturgy of the Church'.

THE ALTERNATIVE SERVICE BOOK 1980

The Book of Common Prayer was (and is) greatly loved by its admirers. But however beautiful the language of the seventeenth century may be, it is not necessarily appropriate for worship in the last half of the twentieth century. Furthermore, criticism could be made of some of the theology found in the Book of Common Prayer. There is also greater appreciation of the principles and structure of liturgy now than there was in those days. It was therefore decided in 1976 that an alternative service book should be provided. A period of experimentation followed, when the Liturgical Commission of the Church of England put forward services, and invited people to comment on them, since the only sensible way to decide whether or not a liturgy is a good liturgy is by trying it out. (The General Synod was involved in the long process of revising draft services in which lay people of course participated.) Finally in 1980 the Alternative Service Book was authorised for use in parish churches, if a Parochial Church Council so decides. The Church of England can therefore pride itself both on having involved lay people in the production of these new services, and on providing new services that are only an alternative to the old prayer book. Nothing is imposed against the will of a congregation, although of course there will usually be some members of a congregation who do not approve of the choice their representatives on the Parochial Church Council have made.

The principles of the Alternative Service Book are described in its preface:

> Rapid social and intellectual changes . . . together with a world-wide reawakening of interest in liturgy, have made it desirable that new understandings of worship should find expression in new forms and styles . . . . The provision of alternative services is to be welcomed as an enrichment of the Church's life rather than as a threat to its integrity. As long ago as 1906 a Royal Commission reported that 'the law of public worship in the Church of England is too narrow for the religious life of the present generation'. Three-quarters of a century later it can be said with even greater certainty that the gospel of the living Christ is too rich in content, and the spiritual needs of his people are too diverse, for a single form of worship to suffice.

THE DIFFERENCES BETWEEN THE TWO BOOKS

The Alternative Service Book is written in modern English which is sometimes pedestrian and which intentionally lacks literary distinction. This is in contrast to the Book of Common Prayer, which is written in the old fashioned literary English of three centuries ago. In the Alternative Service Book God is addressed as 'You' rather than 'Thou'. The old, well known and well loved form of the Lord's Prayer has been translated more accurately into modern English. The services in the new prayer book accord better with the principles of liturgy than the old book (for example in the structure of the Holy Communion). There is an even more fundamental difference of spirituality, and it is this change which has most upset those who were used to the old ways. The Prayer Book concept of God is predominantly a God who is far off, transcendent, all powerful, and to be feared as well as to be loved; while the Alternative Service Book portrays God as more approachable and in our midst. The long and grovelling confession of sins has gone, and its place taken by a more concise but heartfelt statement of repentance. Perhaps the most symbolic difference between the two services of Holy Communion is that the older service was always in the past celebrated with the priest facing eastwards as though God were far off (except in some evangelical churches where the celebrant knelt at the north end of the table), whereas churches which use the new services are now usually ordered with the priest facing the people, as though God was in their midst. There are more positive attitudes to the family in the new baptism service, to sex in the new marriage service, to personal commitment in the new confirmation service, and less emphasis on 'the miseries of this sinful world' (BCP) in the new funeral service. On the other hand the words of the old book had a certain grandeur, reverence and a dignity which seems appropriate when addressing God our Maker and Redeemer, and many people feel this is missing in the new version.

FURTHER AHEAD

The new prayer book was advisedly called 'Alternative Service Book 1980' to emphasise that it was not a permanent alternative to the Prayer Book. It was authorised only for a limited number of years. The Liturgical Commission has been busily preparing more alternative services for use in the revised Alternative Service Book 2000 about which General Synod must in due course decide. No doubt those against any form of change will be against any alteration. But change all around us has been taking place in this century faster than in any other, with the result that new forms may be required to meet changing circumstances.

6

The Church of England by Law Established

The Church of England is 'by law established'. What does this mean?

Sometimes the phrase 'State church' is used to describe it. This may suggest at worst that the State is being divinised, rather like the German church under the Nazis, with its thinly disguised worship of the nation; or at best that the Church is a body set up by the State for formal worship instead of an expression of genuine spirituality. Either of these would be a travesty of the Church of England today.

The phrase 'Church of England as by law established' means that the church is supported or 'established' through legislation. The laws affecting the establishment of the church are many and complex, so much so that it would be a major task to disentangle it, although some laws have been relaxed to enable the Church of England to make its own decisions. For example, a special law is no longer needed to change the boundaries of a parish: the Church has been delegated that power to use as it thinks fit. The establishment of the Church of England today impinges on the ordinary lay person in the following three ways:

• The Crown appoints diocesan bishops and deans of cathedrals.

• While the Church can alter its forms of worship (providing these are consonant with the beliefs of the Book of Common Prayer), any Measure passed by the General Synod still has to have the agreement of both Houses of Parliament.

• All parishioners residing within a parish have certain rights in the parish church (such as to be married there and to have their funerals there).

Some other countries in Europe also have established churches, among them Norway, Sweden and Germany. In some there is even a church tax, although citizens may opt out of it. The Church of England is not supported financially by the State (except, like other churches in Britain, for services rendered as in prison chaplaincies, or for repairs to ancient buildings through the Heritage Fund). Its endowments were all given to it by benefactors in the past.

THE CROWN AND THE CHURCH
Henry VIII ruled the Church, and called himself its supreme head, although he was usually careful to get Parliament to pass his decisions into law. Elizabeth I called herself its supreme governor, although she also was usually careful to seek the approval of Parliament (or of her council acting on its behalf) for any changes that she wished. The 'royal prerogative' still remained, although it was very sparingly used. During the reigns of the Georges, executive power passed from the monarch to the Prime Minister and his cabinet. Today we have a representative monarchy, which acts through Parliament and the Premier. And so when the Crown appoints someone to a church office, the actual decision is made in the Prime Minister's office, and the Sovereign rubberstamps it.

THE LAWS OF THE CHURCH

Any change in the Church's canon law (which is itself part of the law of the land) must not contradict the secular law and must receive the Royal Assent. Any Measure which the Church wishes to introduce, which would make changes in the laws governing the Church, must be approved by Parliament. There is an Ecclesiastical Committee of both Houses of Parliament which pronounces on whether a Measure is expedient or not; and then each House has to vote on the Measure as it stands without any amendment. (This is not so extraordinary as appears at first sight. Other churches, such as the Methodist Church, have decided that, for the sake of the trusteeship of their property, they must seek the agreement of Parliament before any changes can be made in their fundamental articles.)

THE APPOINTMENT OF BISHOPS AND DEANS

The Crown also appoints bishops and deans and certain other dignitaries. This is not unique to the Church of England. The Roman Catholic Church permitted certain bishops to be appointed in this way until the Pope comparatively recently insisted on making all of them his own personal appointments. Although the Crown appoints to a vacant bishopric, it has agreed always to choose one of two names forwarded to it by a church body called the Crown Appointments Commission (see page 38 below). Suffragan bishops (that is to say, assistants to a diocesan bishop) are by tradition appointed by the diocesan bishop concerned. He submits two names to the Crown, making it clear that he wishes the first name to be appointed; and it is.

THE FINANCES OF THE CHURCH OF ENGLAND

Parliament has set up a body called the Church Commissioners (see chapter 17), who deal, among other things, with the Church of England's endowments. This body is nominally accountable to Parliament, in that its annual report is laid on the table of the House of Commons, but no control has ever been exercised over it. More and more of its resources are being channelled into pensions for retired clergy, and so most of the money needed to resource the Church of England is now coming from its living members. It seems likely that the Church of England will have to become self-supporting so far as its running costs are concerned in the foreseeable future.

CREEPING DISESTABLISHMENT

The Church of England over the last 150 years has achieved increasing self-government. In 1853 the Convocations of the provinces of Canterbury and York (which comprised an upper house of bishops and a lower house of clergy representatives) began, after a long interval, to discuss serious church business, although they did not have the power to alter church law. All changes other than canon law had to be initiated by Parliament. In 1885 a house of laity was added in each province. In 1904 all six bodies combined to make a Representative Council. In 1920 this council was superseded by the Church Assembly, which could present Measures to Parliament under the rules outlined above. In 1970 the old Assembly was in turn superseded by the General Synod, in which all three houses of bishops, clergy and laity were joined (with certain reserve powers for the bishops). The revision of canon law was completed by the Church. The Worship and Doctrine Measure gave the Church of England powers to regulate its own worship, provided that the Book of Common Prayer was always an option.

In 1978 a new method of appointing diocesan bishops was initiated. Instead of appointments being made by the Prime Minister after consultation (with enormous power in the hands of a civil servant who was Patronage Secretary), a Crown Appointments Commission of eight persons was set up by General Synod, which was to forward two names to the Crown, expressing its preference if it so wished. It was agreed that the Crown would appoint one of the two names, or if both were unacceptable it would ask the Commission to suggest two more names.

As a result of these changes, the Church of England can regulate its own worship, shortlist two names (but not actually choose) its own bishops, and initiate (but not enact) its own laws. It also appoints some Church Commissioners (the rest being *ex officio* or appointed by the Crown).

ADVANTAGES OF AN ESTABLISHED CHURCH

There are some advantages to the present situation. A State church means that the Christian faith is officially recognised not merely as a personal and private matter for the individual, but also as the source of values and standards which a country should pursue in its public life. To disestablish the church runs the risk that such a step would be taken as a repudiation of these standards and values by the State.

A State church involves the official demarcation of

parishes, in which everyone has the right to attend his or her parish church, and to be married and buried from there. It makes it clear that the Christian faith is for everyone, and not only for a small élite. The parish priest is not there simply to minister to the congregation, but to counsel all in need who ask for help, and to be involved in local civic and community matters. On the other hand, the practice of religion is entirely voluntary, and no one need attend the parish church or any other church.

A State church also gives pastoral opportunities, since parish clergy may visit any household in the parish in the course of their pastoral work. This also provides evangelistic opportunities. It enables the church to communicate with the large number of people who only belong very loosely to the church but who are not without faith.

In an ecumenical age, the Archbishop of Canterbury regularly consults with the leaders of other churches about national church events or matters of national policy. It is fair to say that nowadays church establishment involves more responsibilities than it provides privileges.

The establishment of the Church of England today does not impose any undue restriction on its members compared with those of another church, except, say, that it cannot have bishops appointed of whom the Prime Minister may disapprove.

DISADVANTAGES OF AN ESTABLISHED CHURCH
A church should be able to run its own affairs without State interference. At some future time there may be a government opposed to Christian values

which might impose intolerable restrictions on the Church. In any case if Parliament refused a Measure which the Church of England regarded as vital to its welfare, it would have to demand disestablishment.

In 1928 Parliament refused to legalise a new prayer book (although it must be said that this did not prevent it being used, even in the crypt chapel of the House of Commons). More recently the Ecclesiastical Committee regarded as 'inexpedient' the original Measure which would have allowed a divorced person to be ordained without any searching inquiry, and also rejected a Measure which attempted to simplify the appointment of diocesan bishops. Many MPs are embarrassed at having to agree measures about church affairs, and very few participate in such debates, which are sometimes held at a very late hour and command an unrepresentative attendance.

SOME FURTHER STEPS

The time may soon come when the Crown Appointments Commission submits only one name for a vacancy in a diocesan see. Many would wish to see the same situation for the Church of England as for the Presbyterian Church of Scotland. The latter is recognised by Parliament as the national church of the land. Yet it is not established by law in the same way as the Church of England. Rather, it is 'recognised' by law. Article VI of its 1921 Declaratory Articles (endorsed by Parliament) recognises the divine appointment of the 'civil magistrate' in his own sphere, and the duty of the Church to acknowledge the kingship of Christ over the nations to obey his laws. The Church and State owe mutual duties to each other, but they can determine their own boundaries. However, the history of the Church of England is very different from that of the Scottish Church, and it is more likely that its creeping disestablishment will continue rather than that there will be a sudden change to the Scottish situation.

7

Spirituality in the Church of England

WORSHIP

The spirituality of a church can be seen in the way its public worship is carried out. Care is usually taken over the liturgy, music and ritual of the Church of England so as to promote the worship of God 'in the beauty of holiness'. With so many parish churches all over England, there are obviously some exceptions. Occasionally complaints are made that worship is carelessly led; sometimes it may seem rather dull and boring; cathedral-style worship in which there seems to be no participation by the congregation may suit some kinds of spirituality, but it repels others. Usually, however, worship in the parish church is a real attempt to offer a 'sacrifice of praise and thanksgiving'.

During the second half of this century there has been a great change in worship in the Church of England. In the past Matins and Evensong, the morning and evening services, were the best attended. While the Holy Communion has always been the most important service of the Church, it used to be celebrated as 'the early service' at 8.00 a.m. or (for the elderly) at midday. Nowadays in most churches (including many in the evangelical tradition) the Parish Communion is the main service of the day, and sometimes the only one. Non-communicating attendance at this service is normally confined to those not yet confirmed and the new services encourage a far greater participation by the congregation.

THE MARKS OF SPIRITUALITY

It is impossible (and undesirable) to 'make windows into people's souls'; at the same time it is usually possible to discern the true marks of private spirituality. Many individual members of a congregation not only attend worship regularly and prayerfully, but also regularly read the Bible, make their own private devotions and prayers, conduct their own private self-examination, pray for others as well as themselves, and not only offer to God their love, thanksgiving and penitence but also wrestle with understanding their faith.

DIFFERENT TYPES OF SPIRITUALITY

Different traditions of churchmanship have developed different forms of spirituality, all aimed at the same goal, that is, to grow in the knowledge and love of God and into a deeper relationship with him through Christ in the Spirit.

Evangelical Spirituality

Evangelicals base their spirituality on the Scriptures. Sermons in their churches will be likely to be concerned with scriptural interpretation. Evangelicals, like many other Christians, read a daily passage at home, but they also study the Scriptures and read books about them with a care and earnestness that is not always found elsewhere. They may find strength through attending large conferences and festivals. Some forms of evangelicalism are very informal and appeal to young people, with spirituality expressed in modern worship songs and gospel music and handclapping. In evangelical teaching emphasis will be not only on the Scriptures, but also on the saving death of Jesus, often explained in terms of substitution (Jesus paid the penalty which we deserve). They will also emphasise 'justification through faith' (believers are made right before God not through their own worth or actions, but by faith in the atoning sacrifice of Christ). There is often a simplicity and directness about evangelical worship not always found elsewhere. Evangelicals often attend groups within their parish church for prayer meetings. They pay special attention to the spirituality of young people as they grow up. Some of them are charismatics (people who speak and act under the impulse of the Holy Spirit), and reveal spiritual gifts, such as speaking in an apparently unknown language, at renewal services and meetings. They are usually the most active in sharing the good news of Christ with others and in interceding for others in prayer. Although evangelicals are usually loyal Anglicans, they tend to sit light to church structures, and to share fellowship with evangelicals in other denominations.

Catholic Spirituality

Catholics tend to emphasise the church and the continuity of Christian traditions more than others. They centre most of their worship on the Eucharist. Whereas evangelicals tend to emphasise their religious feelings, catholics often focus on the objectivity of worship, especially in the Eucharist. They tend to find outward things a help to spiritual worship. They use the senses in worship more than most; sight, smell, touch, taste; and they may use forms of spirituality which originated in the Roman Catholic Church, such as the Catholic forms of private prayer. They tend to be specially concerned with the authority of the office of bishop and priest. In their prayers they are likely not to concentrate on petition and intercession so much as on 'the practice of the presence of God', meditation and contemplation. Some people will receive the Holy Communion every day in churches where there is a daily celebration. Although the practice is decreasing, there is also private confession before a priest. In some Anglo-Catholic churches there is the tradition of the rosary (beads which may help people to pray), devotions to Our Lady and the service of Benediction (the use of the reserved sacrament in pronouncing God's blessing). The exposition of the Blessed Sacrament (that is, showing the consecrated elements formally as an aid to adoration) is not unknown. There are also likely to be parochial meetings for members of the congregation who wish to join groups.

Central Churchmanship

A great many parishes would be designated neither evangelical nor catholic nor liberal. They may be 'middle of the road', but most would be happy to be just Church of England. They are content with the *via media* as it now stands and do not want to change its emphases. It is not necessary to belong to one of the movements within the Church of England to be a loyal Anglican!

There are also Liberal Protestants and Liberal Catholics and just Liberals who feel the need to bring their faith up to date by expressing it in ways that can be more easily understood in our contemporary culture. They would regard a passion for truth as no less important than a reverence for tradition, and would hold that this search for truth may be helped by new insights where the Holy Spirit is discerned at work outside the Church. 'Modernist' is paradoxically a somewhat out-dated phrase to indicate someone who is determined to explore the Christian faith in radically new ways.

Mutual Enrichment of Traditions

It would be a mistake to think that a certain type of spirituality is to be found only in one school of churchmanship. For example, the worship of Taizé (a French ecumenical monastic order) has influenced different kinds of churchmanship, as has charismatic worship. Most parishes will have parish groups of some kind for those who wish to join them, especially during Lent. The retreat movement flourishes in all traditions, and most dioceses have either their own retreat house or somewhere else where groups from parishes can go out for quiet, and where parish week-ends can take place.

SUMMARY

Much remains to be done to deepen the spirituality of members of the Church of England, and especially that of 'ordinary' members. In particular there is scope for deepening family spirituality, with habits of family prayers and grace before meals. Nonetheless a genuine spirituality can usually be found in the congregation of almost all parishes in the Church of England and in the homes of many of its members.

8

Saints in the Church of England

A church should be judged partly on its ability to produce saints. 'The saints are lifegivers to their fellows, because they themselves have received life from the Lord and giver of life who dwells within them. All are called to be saints, called to give and receive life, to accept their life as a gift from God, and to offer it back to him in thanksgiving and praise' (A. M. Allchin). Each of the great churches of Christendom has evolved its own traditions of holiness. In the Church of England, as might be expected from its pluralism, there is a considerable variety of holiness among its saints.

HOW SAINTS ARE OFFICIALLY RECOGNISED

The word 'saints' originally referred to all baptised Christians, who are set apart by God to reflect his holiness. The Church has always honoured those who have shown special devotion to God in Christ, and the word 'saint' came to be used to describe them. From the fourth century onwards devotion to the saints spread rapidly. Some early saints were given the title by popular acclaim. Some reputations rested on very slender historical evidence. Between the twelfth and the seventeenth centuries local bishops of the Roman Catholic Church 'beatified' saints for commemoration in their own dioceses. Since then the status of sainthood in the Western Church has been regulated by Rome by a formidable process, including evidence of miracles performed and an 'advocatus diaboli' or devil's advocate (an official who is appointed to argue against the 'beatification' of a particular individual).

PRE-REFORMATION SAINTS

The Book of Common Prayer includes a number of English saints in its lectionary. Some were martyrs, such as Alban (killed by the Romans *c.* 209); Edmund, King and Martyr (870), who refused to share his kingdom with pagan invaders; Edward, King of the West Saxons (978), who was killed unjustly but was hardly a martyr; and Alphege, Archbishop of Canterbury (1012), who was killed by invading Danes. Some were saintly bishops, such as Chad (672), abbot and bishop; Swithun, Bishop of Winchester (862), of whom little is known other than he was counsellor of kings; Dunstan, Archbishop of Canterbury (988), a man of many talents, both secular and spiritual, who reordered monastic life and founded monasteries; Hugh, Bishop of Lincoln (1200), whom John Ruskin described as 'the most beautiful sacerdotal [priestly] figure known to me in history', brave, holy, and a champion of the common people; Richard, Bishop of Chichester (1253), a man of true simplicity and generosity, ruthless against abuse and happy among humble folk. Etheldreda (679) was a saintly woman who founded a nunnery at Ely where the cathedral stands. The Venerable Bede (735) was a monk, historian and 'doctor of the church'. Edward the Confessor (1066) was a king with a general reputation for religious devotion and generosity. Saints and martyrs are commemorated on the day of their death, when they entered into eternal life. There are of course many other saints who do not feature in the Prayer Book calendar, and some of them are observed in local festivals and commemorations.

POST-REFORMATION SAINTS

Since the Reformation only one saint had been added to the Church of England's calendar in the Book of Common Prayer, Charles I, King and Martyr (1649) (and he was added by royal mandate). However, the situation changed with the publication of the Alternative Service Book 1980. There the list was radically revised with many additions and deletions. The resulting calendar of saints was authorised by General Synod; but as the house of bishops had the right to produce the version for approval after final revision, they insisted on the inclusion of Mrs Josephine Butler (1907), described as 'Social Reformer, Wife and Mother'. In fact Mrs Butler befriended prostitutes and managed to get the law repealed according to which they had to be registered.

ENGLISH SAINTS IN THE ALTERNATIVE SERVICE BOOK

The new calendar is ecumenical, including saints from the Roman Catholic and Free Church traditions. Some of these were English pre-Reformation saints: Cuthbert, Bishop of Lindisfarne (missionary bishop of Lindisfarne, a pastor and a solitary and a keen observer of nature, 687); Oswald, King of Northumberland (a Christian convert killed by the pagan Mercians, 642); Aidan (another missionary bishop of Lindisfarne, a pastor and friend of

Oswald, 651); Hilda, Abbess of Whitby (founder of a
monastery both for men and women, counsellor of
kings and ordinary folk, 680); Anselm, Archbishop
of Canterbury (outstanding theologian and philoso-
pher, one of the 'doctors of the Church', 1109);
Thomas Beckett, Archbishop of Canterbury (martyred on the orders of King Henry II, 1170); John
Wyclif, a bold free-thinking theologian and
reformer who initiated a new theological movement
which developed into a popular movement (1384);
and Julian of Norwich (an anchorite who received
mystical visions in her Norwich cell, *c.* 1417). The
inclusion of these names adds to the richness of
England's roll of pre-Reformation saints.

Those from the post-Reformation Church of
England show how the record of sanctity was being
continued in the reformed Church of England.
There are some martyrs: James Hannington, Bishop
of East Equatorial Africa, a missionary (1885);
Thomas Cranmer (appointed Archbishop of
Canterbury by Henry VIII and martyred by Queen
Mary, 1556). There is also the great biblical scholar,
William Tyndale, who translated the Scriptures and
was killed for so doing (1536). Theologians and
divines are among those commemorated, for example Richard Hooker (who wrote quintessential
Anglican theology, 1600); Lancelot Andrewes,
Bishop of Winchester (whose prayers are still used
for meditation today, 1626); Jeremy Taylor, Bishop
of Down and Connor and Pastor (who pioneered
Anglican moral theology, 1667); George Herbert (a
priest who had retired from public life in Cambridge
in order to be ordained – he become a beloved pastor who wrote much loved religious poetry, 1633);

Nicholas Ferrar (who founded a lay order based on his family at Little Gidding and became an example of holiness, 1637); Thomas Ken, Bishop of Bath and Wells (a man of holiness and integrity, who refused to give allegiance to William and Mary so long as King James was alive, and resigned his see, 1711); William Law (a mystic who also refused to swear allegiance, on this occasion to George I after the death of Queen Anne, and whose mystical writings show great power and insight, 1761); William Wilberforce (an evangelical who was a tireless social reformer and whose efforts to abolish slavery were finally successful, 1833); Charles Simeon (an evangelical pastor and preacher at Cambridge who made a profound impression on undergraduates and on the Church generally, 1836); John Keble (a pastor, priest and poet who gave rise to the Oxford Movement through a much publicised sermon on apostasy, 1866). The list of both men and women was deliberately chosen to show the range of devotion and spirituality in the Church of England. Further additions to the church calendar are planned for the revised Alternative Service Book 2000.

OTHER ENGLISH SAINTS

There is of course a multitude of men and women who qualified for admission to the list, and the Liturgical Commission of the Church of England had great difficulty in submitting a list to the General Synod for approval. For example, Henry Vaughan (poet and doctor, 1678), Mary Godolphin (wife and mother of the seventeenth century with a deep spirituality) and Edward King (a very saintly Bishop of Lincoln, the focus of Protestant accusa-

tions, 1910) might well have been included. Many
people have their favourite saint, and it would be
invidious to suggest the names of any alive or only
very recently dead. There are also many local commemorations. To illustrate the wide range of possible local commemorations, it may be of interest that,
when the present writer was Bishop of Birmingham,
he drew up a list of people who had resided in the
diocese for such local observances. These included,
in addition to some of the above, people such as
Charles Gore (first bishop of the diocese, 1932),
John Rogers (martyred under Queen Mary, 1555),
B.F. Westcott (bishop and theologian, 1907), Samuel
Johnson (teacher and writer, 1784), and J.B.
Lightfoot (Bishop of Durham and theologian,
1889).

When the list comes to be revised again, there will
be several candidates for inclusion from the twentieth century; people such as William Temple (archbishop and teacher), Evelyn Underhill (mystic),
Austin Farrer (teacher) and C.S. Lewis (Christian
apologist). The lectionary of the Alternative Service
Book includes, in addition to All Saints' Day, a festi-
val of the Saints and Martyrs of England, which
allows us to make a general commemoration.

SAINTS OF THE CHURCH OF ENGLAND

Lists of saints mean little: it is the details of the lives
of the saints which provide evidence of their holiness and sanctity. The Church of England does not
make claims to great holiness, but it can rejoice in its
record of saints. They include people of personal
holiness, mystics and lovers of God, missionaries,
martyrs and theologians, archbishops and bishops,

teachers, poets and social reformers. There are, of course, many people of hidden holiness, known only to God, to be found in country and urban parishes. It is simply not true to say that the Church of England does not produce saints.

9

Pluralism in the Church of England

The Church of England contains, as we have already noted (see pages 43–46), Catholics, Protestants, liberals and those who prefer not to give themselves any label. Does this make sense?

In the first place, it is unlikely in any church (except perhaps in a small sect) that all its members will entirely agree in their understanding of the Christian faith, although they will of course be united in fundamentals. (You will find similar differences within your own congregation in the parish church.) Differences are to be found too in other churches. For example, there is at present quite a divide between conservatives and liberals in the Roman Catholic Church, but of course there is no talk of any schism. Similarly some Baptist churches overseas are very liberal in their outlook (this is particularly true of New Zealand, where there are many Baptists) whereas in England they tend to be conservative. These differences within one church are due to many factors: the tradition of a particular parish church or chapel, cultural influences on an individual, differences of temperament and so on.

THE INFLUENCE OF THE PRAYER BOOK
The differences between the various church movements in the Church of England have already been described (see pages 43–46). These have at times

given rise to a 'party spirit'. There is a long history of different traditions in the Church of England, which goes right back to the Reformation itself. In the past the Church has been kept united partly through common loyalty to the bishop of a diocese (who is its focus of unity) and also through the unifying influence of the Book of Common Prayer, which was generally used throughout the church. Although there might be great differences of ritual and ceremonial in worship, and although there would be small local alterations in the words of the Prayer Book service, members of one parish congregation joining in the worship of another would recognise the same prayers of the same service at which they were accustomed to worship in their home parish. There was an intentional ambiguity in the wording of some prayers in the Prayer Book when it was composed, so that people could worship together despite holding some differing opinions.

THE ALTERNATIVE SERVICE BOOK

When, in 1980, the Alternative Service Book was authorised for use in public worship, not as a substitute but as an alternative to the Book of Common Prayer, it quickly proved very popular. Since then the Liturgical Commission has issued some other forms of worship for certain services. Most parishes prefer to use this new prayer book, and there are many alternatives in it. All the same, the basic structure of a service is easily discernible, and one of the authorised 'consecration prayers' is almost always used at the Holy Communion. So it can be said even today that one of the unifying factors of the Church of England is the use by people of very different churchmanship of one or other of these prayer books.

THE EARLY CHURCH

There have always been divisions of opinion within the Church. Sometimes these have been quite marked, as for example those which Paul described in the Corinthian church (1 Corinthians 1.10–17), with a Peter and a Paul and even a Christ party. Elsewhere Paul emphasised 'justification by faith' (that is, that we are put in the right with God by appropriating through faith what Christ has done for us). But James in his epistle insists on 'justification by works', pointing out that faith is of little use unless it is translated into action (James 2.14–24). Other instances could be given of divisions of opinion in the primitive church, and these continued throughout early church history. It might even be said that the origins of Catholicism and Protestantism can, in some sense, be traced right back to the apostles Peter and Paul themselves. So the existence of different church movements within the one church is not contrary to Scripture: it is what we actually find in the Scriptures. A conflict of ideas can be fruitful, provided this takes place in a Christian spirit.

CHRISTIAN LOVE

At the heart of the Christian gospel is love: the love of God for us in Christ, and the love which we reflect back to God and to our fellow men and women. This love can show itself within the structures of the church, by a spirit of forbearance and meekness. We do not have to give up our own individual understanding of the truth, but at the same time we accept that others may be just as good, or even better Christians, though they may have a different understanding of the faith. Therefore we can respect one another within the same church, and of course within the same congregation. In any case we are agreed on the fundamentals of the Christian faith even if we may differ over their interpretation or over our differing styles of worship. It is in accordance with this Christian spirit that two people may kneel at the same communion rail side by side to receive the sacrament of the Lord's Supper even though they may have very different understandings of its meaning. They receive the same grace and are bonded together through communion with Christ and with one another.

CHRISTIAN UNITY

As well as love, unity is another fundamental of the gospel. We are all one in Christ, and we are united through our common baptism. It follows therefore that the unity of the people of God is more important than universal agreement on matters of faith. (This is not to deny that there must be some limit to the differences for those authorised to teach the faith or to represent a particular church or denomination.) The Church of England therefore embraces as many people within its membership as will accept its discipline and fundamental beliefs (see pages 21–28). By so doing it is acting in a very proper way and according to biblical principles. As we have seen, when the Elizabethan Settlement was made (page 11), the intention was the Church

of England should be the church of all English
people. That attempt failed; but it was a noble ideal
which should be kept in mind in all re-union
negotiations.

10

The Validity of Anglican Orders: Deacons, Priests and Bishops

Almost all churches, except for the Society of Friends (Quakers), appoint people to lead worship and to take pastoral responsibility for the congregation. Such people are almost always authorised to do this at some formal ceremony. Those in authority are ordained, and become 'ministers of religion'.

DIFFERENCES BETWEEN THE CHURCHES OVER THEIR ORDAINED MINISTERS

Many churches, Protestant as well as Catholic, ordain their ministers with prayer and the laying on of hands. Most Protestant churches ordain people as 'ministers' and reject the word 'priest'. (The word was originally 'presbyter', meaning 'elder', but it has what are for them the undesirable connotations of Old Testament priesthood.)

Few Protestant churches have bishops. Few of them lay claim to the 'apostolic succession' in the laying on of hands (that is to say, a succession of ordination going back to very early days). Presbyterians, who almost universally reject bishops, may claim that the apostolic succession is through the minister, whom they regard as the equivalent of a bishop in the early church. The Methodists could make a similar claim, since their orders stem from John Wesley, an ordained Anglican priest.

The Church of England, however, at its Reformation retained what was universal in the early church: the threefold order of bishops, priests and deacons. The preface to the ordinal in the Book of Common Prayer makes it clear that these offices are to be continued in the Church of England with the laying on of hands, and a sermon is required at the ordination of deacons and priests to show how 'necessary' that order is to the Church. In the sixteenth and seventeenth centuries 'necessary' could mean 'useful'. The word priest, rather than presbyter, was deliberately retained.

CHANGES AT THE REFORMATION AND THE RESTORATION

Before Elizabeth I restored the Church of England after her accession to the throne, Mary her predecessor had reconciled the English church with Rome. Great care however was taken to ordain Parker, Elizabeth's Archbishop of Canterbury, with a sufficient number of other bishops laying hands on him to ensure that his consecration was regular and valid, although it was not so in Roman Catholic eyes because it lacked the consent of the Pope. (The story that he was privately ordained at the Nag's Head Tavern is a myth which no one now believes: if you have ever heard about it, forget it.) Again, when the period of the Commonwealth ended, and the Church of England was reinstated at the Restoration, there were just sufficient former bishops to be found who could ensure proper continuity in the consecration of new bishops, so that the outward sign of apostolic succession could be properly attested as well as its inner reality. Bishops and priests of the Church of England continue the same functions as they carried out in the early church, and are ordained not only with the outward signs but also with the same intention as they were. However their orders are not regarded as valid by the Roman Catholic Church, although official Roman Catholic teaching now affirms that the Anglican priesthood is a real ministry which bears fruits of grace, even if it cannot be called the office of priesthood as Rome understands it (see Appendix). This may be paralleled by Anglicans' glad acceptance that non-episcopally ordained Free Church ministers carry out a real and efficacious ministry of word and sacraments.

Anglicans can have full confidence in the validity of their threefold order of bishops, priests and deacons. Their doctrine of holy orders is characteristic of Anglican reformed Catholicism. A pastoral description of the work and function of deacons, priests and bishops can be found in the 1662 Prayer Book, and in more contemporary language in the various ordination services in the Alternative Service Prayer Book.

I have summarised Roman Catholic objections to Anglican orders and their refutation in an appendix after the last chapter of the book.

11

Anglicans and the Ordination of Women to the Priesthood

Since 1994 the Church of England, after many years of debate, has followed other provinces of the Anglican Communion (such as Canada, New Zealand and the United States) by ordaining women to the priesthood. Women had already been ordained as ministers of religion by Lutherans, Methodists, Congregationalists, United Reformed and Baptists. Before women in the Church of England could be ordained, a vote with more than a two-thirds majority in favour was required among laity, clergy and bishops in the General Synod. The matter had already been referred to the dioceses for their opinions.

The Roman Catholic and Orthodox churches, in their official pronouncements, are strongly opposed to the ordination of women, as too are a good many Anglicans still today. What are the objections to this move, and how are these objections met?

☐ Some say that the Church of England has no authority to make a unilateral move of such importance without the agreement of the whole Western Church. However, there is no prospect of an ecumenical conference of all the churches, and so this agreement could not be obtained. Furthermore, if the Church of England went its own way apart from the Church of Rome at the Reformation, that was a far greater step than ordaining women to the priesthood. It affirmed at the Reformation its authority to make its own decisions without waiting for the rest of the Western church to agree.

❏ Some Roman Catholics say that only men can act in the person of Christ. But priests do not impersonate Christ, they represent him; and women can do this as well as men. St Paul recognised that 'in Christ there is neither male or female'. The Christian belief is that God assumed humanity rather than that he became a person of the male gender. This is made clear in the Nicene Creed in which the Greek word for a human being (*anthropos*) rather than a male (*aner*) is used.

❏ It is said that since Jesus deliberately did not choose to include women among the Twelve, so the Church ought also deliberately not choose them as successors of the Twelve. However, Jesus only chose Jews to be among the Twelve, and no one suggests that Gentiles (non-Jews) should not be priests. In any case there were no successors to the Twelve Apostles, other than Matthias, although there were apostolic men, like Andronicus and Junia(s) in Rome (Romans 16.7), the latter of whom may even have been a woman. But Jesus could not have chosen a woman among the Twelve, because in those days in Galilee and Judaea her authority would not have been respected. It is only recently that the changing status of women has enabled their authority to be recognised, for example as political leaders, and the same is true for women as priests.

❏ Some evangelicals say that St Paul called man

'the head' of a woman (1 Corinthians 11.3) and that women have a God-given inferiority to men. In fact the Greek word for head can mean either 'origin' or 'the head' in contrast to other parts of the body, but never the directing force. In this particular passage it seems to refer to origin, with a reference to Eve who was fashioned, according to Genesis, from Adam's rib. Nonetheless there are certainly references elsewhere in the New Testament to the inferiority of women, with the requirement that women be submissive to their husbands; but these, like injunctions to wear modest attire and head coverings, follow Jewish customs of the time: they are cultural conventions, not divine commands.

☐ Some people have alleged that if a woman is a priest, there is confusion of symbolism, with a woman speaking in the name of the Son. However, the Church is characterised in the New Testament by female symbolism, and there is no confusion in a male priest speaking in the name of the Church.

There are of course positive arguments in favour of women priests as well as those which contradict the arguments of those who oppose them.

☐ Women may experience a vocation to the priesthood which, when tested by the same criteria as a man's vocation, appears to be just as genuine.

☐ A priest not only represents God to men and women, but also men and women to God. In our present culture many women find it difficult to feel that they are truly represented before God by men only. It is necessary nowadays for representation to be by both men and women.

☐ Men and women complement each other in the priesthood. While there is no absolute stereotype, many women have skills which men lack. There is a wholeness when they are both working together.

THE 'TWO INTEGRITIES'

There was opposition from nearly one-third of the members of the General Synod to the ordination of women to the priesthood. Opponents, generally speaking, were either catholics who believed that such a move is contrary to the traditions of the Church, or evangelicals who believed that it is contrary to scriptural teaching to give a woman the authority of a priest. By 1996 some 500 full-time priests of the Church of England are expected to have left the Church of England as a result, but in no case has the majority of a congregation gone with them. Some parishes which are opposed to women priests and who object to their diocesan bishops ordaining them are now served by Provincial Episcopal Visitors (popularly called 'flying bishops'), that is to say, bishops who are also opposed to women priests and who work under the diocesan bishop, but who are licensed by the archbishops. An 'Act of Synod' protects the position of priests who oppose women priests as *bona fide* members of the Church of England, and recognises that there are 'two integrities'. In other words, members of the Church of England may disagree with these ordinations, and still be loyal members of the Church, and clergy of both views are equally eligible for higher office in the church. There are safeguards, too, for those bishops who were opposed to their ordination when women were first ordained, and for those parishes which have decided that they do not wish to have a vicar or curate who is a woman. While these arrangements certainly strain the unity of the church, they nonetheless serve to keep it united.

BISHOPS
Women are not eligible, under the present Measure, to become bishops.

12

The Clergy of the Church of England

Some 99 per cent of a church consists of laity. Each member of the laity is as important in the eyes of God as any one of the clergy. Nonetheless the clergy have an importance out of proportion to their number, in so much as they are authorised to preach the word of God and to administer the sacraments, and they provide leadership to the Church and pastoral oversight. Thus they are essential to the functioning of the Church. The number of Anglican clergy peaked during the end of the Victorian era. In 1901 there were 23,781 clergy for a population of 30.7 million. In those days ordinands were drawn almost exclusively from one social class. Residential training of clergy had begun (in theological colleges), but there was no selection procedure other than the bishop's decision. Today the position has greatly changed. At the end of 1993, nearly a century after the 1901 census, there was a total of 12,294 clergy (men and women) in the Church of England for a population of 48.3 million.

THE TRAINING OF ANGLICAN CLERGY IN THE TWENTIETH CENTURY

Nowadays there is a selection procedure. All candidates have to attend a residential selection conference where they are assessed; and although a bishop is not bound to take the recommendations of the conference, no grant for training is forthcoming

from the Church unless the candidate has attended.
The provision of these grants is a major burden on
the Church of England: the 1995 budget has set
aside over £6 million from church collections for
this purpose.

During training there is a syllabus of subjects for
study; and assessments must be made or examina-
tions passed before ordination. The training also
concentrates on spiritual formation in the ministry.
Of those attending a selection conference in 1992,
52 per cent were recommended or conditionally
recommended. The sponsoring diocese usually
recommends a parish for their first job, where they
'serve their title'. They are ordained as deacons
(during which time they learn in practice on the
ground) and a year later as priests. Whereas in the
past the market favoured deacons looking for place-
ments, nowadays as a result of financial stringency
theological students do not always find it easy to find
a vacancy (see page 91).

During 1992 347 men and women were ordained
as deacons. There is some cause for concern over
the low number of really outstanding men and
women coming forward, although selection procedures are generally successful in recommending
only those who will make really good and con-
scientious priests.

The average age of those ordained in 1993 was just
under 35 for men and three years older for women.
One of the characteristics of ordinands at the end of
the twentieth century is the preponderance of older
people being ordained. While they bring with them
experience of the world, they do not always have the
theological knowledge and competence of those

who have read theology at a university before proceeding to ordination.

CLERGY STATISTICS

During 1994 there was an extraordinary increase of ordinations to the priesthood, as over 1,000 women, who already had been ordained deacon, were admitted to the priesthood. Since they were already serving as ministers of religion, they did not really increase the number of clergy in the Church of England. In other countries where the Anglican Church has already ordained women to the priesthood, the result has been an increase in the number of women coming forward for ordination, and this is also to be expected in England.

A distinction must be made between clergy who receive a stipend from the Church and those who work as priests but are paid by an outside body (for example, school or hospital chaplains, or chaplains in the armed services). A few clergy are in secular jobs. Some are ordained to the non-stipendiary ministry; that is to say, they earn their living in a secular post, and exercise their priesthood partly in their secular job, and partly in a parochial ministry during their 'free time'. Other non-stipendiaries, especially women priests, work full-time. Non-stipendiaries have to be over 30 years of age, and some of them are pensioners. A few of these are ordained only to a 'local' ministry.

At the end of 1993 there were 10,080 men and 737 women working in the full-time ordained ministry of the Church of England, a total of 10,817. (There are some 13,000 parishes in the Church of England.) The balance of 1,487 clergy (to make up the grand total of 12,294) are 'licensed' (that is, they are working with the approval of the bishop) as chaplains in the armed forces, in education, in the prison service or elsewhere, or serving in non-diocesan posts, or working in non-stipendiary or local ministry.

RESIGNATIONS

By 1993 215 clergy had resigned from full-time ministry in the Church of England because of the ordination of women to the priesthood. Between 1994 and 1997 it is expected that 285 more will resign, making a total of 500, less than 4 per cent of the total number of clergy.

In any case there is a slight annual decline in the total number of ordained ministry despite the numbers being ordained. This is because of the age structure of the clergy, and for this reason the decline is likely to continue. In the past, however, probably too many clergy were ordained. The present situation enables more lay people to use their talents more fully and to exercise authority in the local congregation.

13

The Laity

The word laity is derived from the Greek word *laos* (meaning 'people'), referring not to the laity in contrast to the clergy, but to the whole 'people of God'. The way in which bishops, clergy and laity now work together is a restoration of an ancient harmony.

In some churches (for example, the Congregational Church) the laity seem to be ultimately in charge, paying and hiring their minister. In such churches, therefore, the laity have very great power, and this is typical of many Protestant churches. In other communions the laity have very little power. For example in the Roman Catholic Church it is not obligatory anywhere to have parish councils, the laity have no say in the choice of their priest, and so far as doctrine is concerned, their task is to 'receive' it, not to participate in its formulation.

The Church of England is both Catholic and reformed, so we might expect a position somewhere between these two extremes; and indeed this is what we find. For example, the laity need to be consulted before a new priest is appointed to a parish. The laity participate in all the work of the General Synod. At the same time very considerable power and influence remain in the hands of the bishop. It is the same at parish level, where the minister has very considerable power and influence, but decision-making is carried out in consultation with representatives of the congregation. This reflects the New Testament church, as when the decision to admit Gentiles was made by the Apostles at a gathering of all the people.

AT THE PARISH LEVEL

At the annual meeting of the parish the priest in charge must give an account of parish life during the past year. Lay officers (churchwardens) are elected by lay members of the parish. Men and women are equally eligible. A Parochial Church Council is elected, which shares with the priest responsibility for the wellbeing of the parish. It is also responsible for its budget, and appoints the other lay officers. Although the conduct of services is the responsibility of the minister, the Parochial Church Council must decide on which services are used (the Book of Common Prayer or the Alternative Service Book). The vicar will normally consult his Council over all matters of policy in the parish, and it often has a series of committees for various aspects of the life of the parish (social, finance and fabric, missionary work and so on).

AT THE DEANERY AND DIOCESAN LEVELS

Representatives elected by their parishes, together with the clergy, form the Deanery Synod, but as this body has no executive power, it is often poorly attended. Representatives from the deanery, lay and clerical, are elected to form the Diocesan Synod. The diocese takes executive action through 'the bishop in synod', that is to say, the bishop sitting with his clergy and lay representatives. Some powers are reserved to the bishop. If a 'vote by houses' is required (namely, the house of bishops, house of clergy and house of laity, all voting separately) the lay members of a synod can block a resolution. The financial matters of a diocese are decided by elected clergy and lay people sitting in a Board of Finance (or a similar body called by some other name). Thus lay people play a full part.

AT NATIONAL LEVEL

Representatives from the Deanery Synod are elected to the General Synod, where matters concerning doctrine are decided, financial decisions are taken, and the policy of the Church of England is decided. Here again the 'house of laity' can block resolutions of which they disapprove, if a vote is required by houses. Lay representatives participate fully in debates concerning new canons (laws) for the church. All boards and commissions of the Synod have lay members. Although each member of each 'house' has an equal vote, the house of bishops is responsible for the final wording of Measures concerning doctrine or worship passed by Synod. It can therefore decide what will be included and what will be excluded from such a Measure, but it cannot ensure that it will be passed by the Synod.

SUMMARY

There is a nice balance between laity, clergy and bishops in the Church of England. Most of the clergy's stipends now come from the giving of the laity. But the money is not given to them direct: it comes through the Church Commissioners. Lay members can introduce private member's motions in synods, or be invited to introduce official legislation. They may and do take the chair at sessions of Deanery, Diocesan or General Synods. At the same time the clergy may be required to meet together at times on their own (in 'Convocation'), and bishops have many powers of appointment, discipline and so on which are not the concern of synods.

14

The Moral Teaching of the Church of England

Life nowadays is very complex, and individuals often find themselves confronted by difficult personal decisions. The Church of England does not attempt to produce moral guidelines to cover all the eventualities of life, because that would be impossible. In any case, different circumstances may demand different moral decisions. A church with a more centralised view of authority, like the Roman Catholic Church, which has an extended list of activities which are 'intrinsically evil' and which no mitigating circumstances can justify, has a greater incentive for detailed guidance. In its catechisms and encyclicals, therefore, it provides authoritative detailed moral rules of behaviour for many situations. Other churches, notably the Protestant churches, tend to leave moral decisions entirely to the individual to be decided by the inspiration of the Holy Spirit, or by reference to the Scriptures, or by the person's conscience; and there is little if any official church guidance.

The Church of England here, as in so much else, holds a middle position. It offers some definite moral guidance, but it also leaves a lot for the individual to decide in good conscience, taking account of the particular circumstances of the case. It also recognises that some moral questions are very difficult to resolve definitively, and that it is therefore quite legitimate for contradictory viewpoints to co-exist within the church (for example, on the subject of pacifism). The Church of England, like all other churches, regards a person's conscience as the supreme arbiter. We all have a duty to follow our conscience, even in those cases where our conscience is in error. At the same time we have a duty to see that our conscience is properly 'informed', so that it is less likely to mislead us. We must take into account the morality of an action, the intention of the agent, and the probable consequences of the act, as well as the traditional teaching of the church and any guidance that Holy Scripture can give us.

THE TEN COMMANDMENTS

We have already seen that the Ten Commandments form part of the catechism. They also form part of the liturgy of the Church, both in the Prayer Book Communion service, and also as an option in the Order for Holy Communion in the Alternative Service Book. They are however somewhat negative in form. The Alternative Service Book, in one of its options, offers a positive scriptural commandment alongside each negative injunction of the Ten Commandments (for example, the command not to dishonour the name of God is followed by the command to worship him with awe and reverence). Another alternative is the use of the 'two great commandments', found both in the Old Testament and in the teaching of Jesus: to love God with our whole being, and to love our neighbours as ourselves.

THE CATECHISM

The catechism not only contains the Ten Commandments, but also contains passages about our duty to God and our duty to our neighbours. It is worth quoting the original words of the old catechism as set out in the Book of Common Prayer, because it shows how moral teaching needs to be kept up to date as culture changes:

> My duty towards my Neighbour, is to love him as myself, and to do to all men, as I would they should do unto me: To love, honour, and succour my father and mother: To honour and obey the Queen, and all that are put in authority under her: To submit myself to all my governors, teachers, spiritual pastors and masters: To order myself lowly and reverently to all my betters: To hurt no body by word or deed: To be true and just in all my dealing: To bear no malice nor hatred in my heart: To keep my hands from picking and stealing, and my tongue from evil-speaking, lying, and slandering: To keep my body in temperance, soberness, and chastity: Not to covet nor desire other men's goods; but to learn and labour truly to get mine own living, and to do my duty in that state of life, unto which it shall please God to call me.

The moral teaching here is permanent, but it is couched in language which shows priorities belonging to an earlier century. For example, there is an emphasis on obedience rather than on participation. There is at least a suggestion that people should not aspire to better themselves. Injunctions against 'picking and stealing' seem to be directed to the labouring classes: there is nothing here about fraud, double dealing, or even bullying. If the catechism were to be rewritten today (and there has been a later revision of it) it would contain the same moral teaching, but it would be expressed in different language and with not quite the same priorities.

THE BOARD FOR SOCIAL RESPONSIBILITY

The General Synod's Board for Social Responsibility has produced reports on many moral issues. These reports, while they have only the authority of the Board that produced them (unless they have been agreed by the Synod after debate) are helpful in giving moral guidance on difficult matters, especially those questions which did not arise in biblical times or in earlier centuries. Among the items covered in these reports are the use of nuclear weapons, gambling, suicide, capital punishment, and moral questions of human sexuality (divorce and remarriage after divorce, contraception, abortion, homosexuality, sterilisation, and questions of human embryology and fertilisation).

GENERAL SYNOD

Many of the moral questions listed above have been the subject of debate in General Synod. Although a vote in General Synod does not in itself alter the moral status of an action, it does, as we have seen, play a significant part in the disseminated authority by which the Church of England finds the will of God for human actions.

THE HOUSE OF BISHOPS

The bishops of the Church of England occasionally issue a statement on ethical issues. For example they issued one in 1991 on homosexuality. But they did not claim that their statement was an authoritative pronouncement binding on the Church. In fact they stated that they had not written the last word on the subject. At the same time their views form an important part of the Church of England's disseminated authority referred to in chapter 3.

DOUBTFUL CASES

There are some cases on which Anglicans are divided, such as whether divorce and remarriage after divorce can ever be justified, whether there are any circumstances in which it is right to have an abortion, and whether two persons with a homosexual orientation can rightly have a permanent, loving and sexual relationship. Although opposing sides may be strong in their convictions, it must be said that the very fact of division shows that the will of God has not yet been clearly recognised in these issues for an authoritative pronouncement to be made. This division of opinion cannot however be regarded as purely negative. When authoritative statements are made which may not be contradicted, moral thinking may be frustrated or stifled. But when contrary views are held, providing each side respects the other, this conflict can be creative.

15

The Church of England and Education

THE IMPORTANCE OF EDUCATION FOR THE CHURCH

Why is the Church concerned with education? Because education is not merely a matter of learning facts and skills, and being taught to think straight; it also inducts young people into the traditions and culture of their country, and so it includes religion. Christians are particularly concerned with education because of the formative influence it has on the values, beliefs and character of young people at a very impressionable age. Religious education in schools should be distinguished from Christian nurture at home and in Sunday schools. Religious education is concerned with teaching young people *about* religion. Christian nurture is about helping them to develop and grow in their own Christian faith.

PAST HISTORY

'Our schools were the creation of the Church, and took their rise at the same time as the introduction of Christianity to this island' (S. J. Curtis). In Britain 'education was the creature of religion, the school was an adjunct of the Church, and the schoolmaster was an ecclesiastical officer' (A. F. Leach). This situation lasted roughly from the seventh to the seventeenth century. In the Middle Ages schools were regulated by the chancellor of the cathedral, and until 1650 all schoolmasters were clergy. Formal education tended to be reserved for the church, the law and the land-owning classes. At the Renaissance and the Reformation, the number of schools increased, and the syllabus widened. In the seventeenth century the first beginnings of a national education can be found, when the Society for Promoting Christian Knowledge (SPCK) began to establish charity schools throughout Britain; and by 1760 30,000 children were being educated in them. By 1787 the number had increased to a quarter of a million.

In the nineteenth century two church societies, one Quaker and one Anglican, had greatly increased this provision. For example, between 1839 and 1869 £24 million (a large sum at nineteenth century prices) was spent on elementary education, of which £15 million was provided by voluntary contributions through the churches. The state began to make grants from the middle of the century. The Church pioneered teacher training colleges in 1840. However, all this was insufficient to provide universal education. The Elementary Education Act of 1870 authorised aid to voluntary schools, and the provision of board schools to fill the gaps. In the voluntary schools, religious education continued to be denominational, but in the board schools it was to be non-denominational. Voluntary schools continued to grow in number. The subsequent history of education is complex, and was accompanied by much dissension, not least on religious issues.

EDUCATION TODAY
The Butler Act of 1944 restructured the educational

system and ended controversy; and although it has been amended by many Education Acts, the basic structure still holds for today. Secondary education was to be provided for all. Voluntary schools remained, and they were divided into two types. One is 'voluntary aided schools' which have two-thirds of their managers appointed by the Church, and the remaining third by the local authority. Religious education and worship is fully denominational, although in practice the 'agreed syllabus' is used for religious education (agreed between the churches and the local authority). The Church, with the aid of a very generous grant, is responsible for the provision of the site and buildings and their maintenance, and for external repairs. All other expenses, including the salaries of the staff, are paid for by the State. In the second type, 'voluntary controlled schools', only one-third of the managers is appointed by the Church. Religious education is according to the agreed syllabus, but the daily act of worship may be fully denominational. For this type of school all the expenditure is met by the State. (Recently schools have been allowed to 'opt out' of local authority supervision and draw their money direct from the Ministry of Education, which some Church of England schools have chosen to do.) Because elementary education came before secondary education, the Church of England has far more junior and infant schools than it has secondary schools. Seventeen in every 100 children in primary education go to church schools, of which the Church of England has over 4,500: 1,913 aided, and 2,740 controlled. Altogether there were 815,322 boys and girls in Church of England primary and secondary schools in 1993, 11.9 per cent of the total for England.

The Church of England also has ten of its own Teacher Training Colleges, a greatly reduced number since many training colleges were closed some years ago. Naturally there is a special emphasis on training teachers for religious education, although these colleges have become very open institutions which transmit to their students little in the way of evangelistic conviction. The need for Christian teachers is very great, especially for teaching religious education, but the Church does not recruit these teachers specially because there is no guarantee that once they are qualified they will be able to teach the subject. The deployment of teachers is in the hands of the headteacher, who may be opposed to religious education, even though there is required to be one lesson a week on the subject, as well as a daily act of worship in school assembly.

THE CHURCH OF ENGLAND'S EXPERTISE IN EDUCATION

Because of its long history and large stake in education, the Church of England has established specialist bodies concerned with education. The Board of Education, through its chairman in the House of Lords, has assisted in the formulation of successive Education Acts, while the National Society (Church of England) for Promoting Religious Education encourages and promotes the teaching of religious education and runs resource centres for this purpose.

THE IMPORTANCE OF CHURCH SCHOOLS

Church schools are generally speaking very popular

with parents, for many reasons. They are often small, their teachers are dedicated, and they may be somewhat traditional in their teaching methods. Parents know that their children will have a real grounding in the Christian religion and moral behaviour. (This is not to pass any judgment on the excellence of many of the State's 'county schools', in religious education or in other matters: it is simply an assessment of church schools' popularity among parents.) So far as the Church is concerned, the schools are particularly valuable. Christian nurture in Sunday schools is important, and so are youth clubs, although these are generally less popular than they once were; and, of course, there are university chaplaincies. But church schools are, generally speaking, the only means of contact that the church has with large numbers of the younger generation today. The local vicar or rector, while he cannot teach religious education in the school (unless he is a qualified teacher), can be invited to speak by the headteacher. He is likely to be the chairman of the governors of a voluntary aided Church of England school. He will have pastoral opportunities through his relationships with parents and their families, and the school often has formal contacts with the local church. These remarks apply mainly to primary schools. The church secondary schools are much larger, and the pastoral opportunities are more limited.

16

The Finances of the Church of England

People realise that a church needs money to keep going, but so far as the Church of England is concerned, the situation is so complicated and the endowments are thought to be so large (not to mention the quite false idea that the State pays money to the church), that there is considerable confusion on the matter.

The Church of England is not only part of a divine society inspired by the Holy Spirit of God to promote God's kingdom on earth through Jesus Christ: it is also a human institution, owning property on trust for the nation, with responsibilities to clergy and lay persons and for the care and maintenance of church buildings for worship. In order to do this, money is needed. In order to understand the present situation, it is necessary to go into a certain degree of detail in what is a complex subject; some readers may prefer to read instead just the conclusion of this chapter

PAST FINANCES OF THE CHURCH

Originally in the earliest days of the Church in England, the local lord of the manor or squire gave land for the church and provided for the priest. More gifts of land or money were in time given to the church, providing an endowment; and in an agricultural era clergy income was enhanced by 'tithes', or one-tenth of the produce of the land, which had to be given to the parish priest. These 'endowments' of the parish were usually quite sufficient to keep the parish priest and, after the Reformation, his family, when priests were allowed to marry. Absentee rectors or vicars often employed curates for a pittance. So among the clergy there were two classes, the rich and the poor. It was permissible in those days to hold more than one 'living', as it was called, and while this may have been justified if one of the parishes was badly endowed, it was also an abuse which increased the wealth of some clergy to the detriment of the Church. In those days it was not even customary to have collections at church services, except on special occasions: the Church of England lived on its inheritance, and the parish maintained the building. This state of affairs lasted until the Victorian era, when many new churches were built and parishes formed, some without any endowment. In an earlier pre-industrial age the parish and the patron of the living between them were responsible for the upkeep of the parish church, and the clergy lived off their endowments and tithe; many of them had 'glebe land' which they used for their own cattle or let out to farmers.

Some bishoprics and some cathedral chapters (that is to say, the bodies in charge of cathedrals) were enormously wealthy, and some very poor. The situation was so anomalous for a Christian body that Prime Minister Robert Peel determined to do something about it. The result was an Ecclesiastical Commission which was intended to make things more fair. This body lasted from 1835 until 1948 and managed the estates and revenues of the Church of England. It was then merged with 'Queen Anne's

Bounty', a fund which had been set up by Queen Anne in 1704 consisting of the first year's revenue of a benefice which used to be given to the Pope and which Henry VIII had confiscated. Queen Anne had directed that the money should be used to augment the livings of the poorer clergy. The new amalgamated body is known at the Church Commissioners.

PRESENT FINANCES OF THE CHURCH

Today matters are much more complex. The Church of England has a central bureaucracy or 'curia' at Church House, Westminster. This has to be paid for. Bishops used to run their dioceses more or less single-handed, but now a diocesan bureaucracy is also needed. Synods have to be serviced and paid for. More bishoprics have been formed and more suffragan (assistant) bishops are needed. Clergy are needed for pastoral and priestly work outside the parish system. Pensions (which used to be paid for by a former incumbent retaining a third of the endowment) needed to be funded and increased to keep pace with inflation. In modern times, the endowment income of a parish (say £200 a year), which was once quite sufficient to keep a priest and his family, became hopelessly inadequate. With new housing and housing estates, many more parishes have been formed without any endowment. In urban areas tithes were non-existent, while protests in rural areas caused them to be commuted. Parish priests, who used to farm their own glebe, now found this impracticable.

A great deal more money is now needed from the living church as well as the money given by people who are long since dead.

THE INCOME OF BISHOPS

The Church Commissioners took over all the estates and endowments of the diocesan bishops. In return for this, they covenanted to provide the bishops with a stipend appropriate to their office (£24,200 for a diocesan bishop in 1993), to provide and maintain a suitable house in which to live rent-free, and certain expenses and allowances needed for the performance of their duties.

The total cost of all this in 1993 was £6.7 million.

THE INCOME OF THE PAROCHIAL CLERGY

A clergyman does not receive a salary (payment for work done) but a stipend (sufficient money on which a family can live and enable the priest to do the job). The Church Commissioners, acting as the Central Stipends Authority, fix a range of stipend payments for a current year, taking into account the inflation rate and average incomes. It pays the clergy's Council Tax and National Insurance and provides and maintains a house rent-free. The parish is responsible for paying necessary clergy expenses. Parsonage houses do not belong to the parish: they are held on a separate kind of trust, and remain the property of parish priests so long as they remain in their posts. Clergy cannot be removed from a 'benefice' (except for a misdemeanour) until they retire, some time between the age of 65 and 70. This is known as the 'parson's freehold'.

Clergy receive 'fees' for weddings, funerals and certain other work. These fees are now in most cases swallowed up in the augmentation received from the church to make up a stipend (the national average for an incumbent in 1993–4 was £12,830). Of this

43 per cent came from parish contributions, 37 per cent from the Church Commissioners, and 20 per cent from fees, glebe rents, etc. Their church pension (when the state pension is added to it) is calculated at two-thirds of their stipend.

THE EXPENSES OF RUNNING A PARISH CHURCH

Maintenance of the fabric is a charge on the parish, apart from the chancel (that part of the church beyond the nave or main part of the church), which is the responsibility of the 'patron'. All the other expenses of the parish church and costs involved in maintaining a church hall also fall on the parish. All churches contribute to the stipends of the clergy through a voluntary system of taxation at diocesan level, known as the 'quota' or 'apportionment'. This is based on average Sunday attendance and (usually) the parish potential. (The total expenditure of the diocese, apart from its endowment income and Church Commissioners' grants, is 'apportioned' fairly among all the parishes as a 'quota' in accordance with their ability to pay.) This enables strong parishes to help weak inner city parishes. It also pays for the diocesan staff, and part goes towards the costs of the General Synod and its boards and committees.

DIOCESAN EXPENSES

These are met by means of the quota or apportionment, and from the income from capital sums and glebe property managed by the diocese. The diocese also pays also for the servicing of the Diocesan Synod and necessary committees and for non-parochial clergy in the diocese.

CATHEDRALS

In 1993 cathedrals received grants totalling £3.1 million from the Church Commissioners. Out of a total annual expenditure of about £40 million, 46 per cent was used for building upkeep and maintenance. At the moment cathedrals just manage to hold their own. But out of a total of 42 cathedrals only 33 were able to make forward projections, and only ten of them anticipate a surplus after restoration expenditure estimated at £29.5 million. Through English Heritage the State makes some contribution to the maintenance of cathedrals and ancient churches as historic buildings, and their chapters are active in raising money. Major appeals have been successful (for example, the £10 million raised by Ely), which suggests good public support. But the Church Commissioners will certainly have to reduce their allocations, and may have to end them. For cathedrals, the future looks uncomfortable.

THE CENTRAL BOARD OF FINANCE

This is the body which is responsible for servicing the General Synod and its various necessary boards and committees (including grants to ordination candidates in theological colleges, the main expense in its budget), and it is accountable to General Synod. It receives most of its contributions from the dioceses by a system of voluntary taxation and its budget for 1993 was over £14 million.

THE CHURCH COMMISSIONERS

The Church Commissioners (with a staff of 283 in 1993) are at present responsible for the management of the main resources of the Church of

England. On 31 December 1993 their capital assets in land and securities amounted to £2,654.2 million, and their net income for the year was £154.9 million. As a result of some property speculation, the value of these assets had dropped by £800 million, but in 1993 some £300 million of this had been recovered. (Since the discovery of this state of affairs, alternative arrangements have been made by the Commissioners to prevent a recurrence of this loss, and to implement better management of their assets.) This, added to increasing pension commitments and the authorisation of grants in excess of income, has resulted in a drop of allocations to dioceses for clergy stipends of £5.5 million in 1994, with continuing reductions in succeeding years. By 2020 all their funds allocated to clergy, it is calculated, will be used for their pensions unless alternative methods of funding are devised. The Church of England, like most other churches, will have to rely increasingly on its living members to pay its way.

The Church Commissioners also have a wide range of responsibilities, in addition to those mentioned above, in connection with redundant churches, pastoral reorganisation schemes, and the functioning of the Pastoral Measure (a complex and wide ranging measure permitting alterations to be made in the pastoral organisation of dioceses, deaneries and parishes). They make contributions to the running of various church bodies such as the Church Urban Fund (the distribution of grants for special projects in needy areas from moneys collected in parishes). They pay in full for the servicing, among others, of the Church's Pensions Board and the Advisory Board for Redundant Churches.

It is possible that the whole position may radically alter and much of the work of the Church Commissioners may be delegated to dioceses, after the Committee set up by the Archbishop of Canterbury to look into the administration of the Church of England and its finances reports in 1995.

CONCLUSION

The Church of England in 1993 needed about £633 million in all to run itself. Of this huge sum, parishes contributed £359 million, the Church Commissioners £155 million, other investment income £90 million, fees and part-time chaplaincies £18 million, and State aid for church buildings £11 million. Although heavier demands will be made on parishes in succeeding years because the Commissioners will need to make smaller allocations to ensure sustainable income, and because of the increasing cost of pensions, it should be well within the grasp of the Church of England to continue to pay its way (apart perhaps for cathedrals if they have huge structural repair bills). The average net giving of members is only £3.42 per week, compared with the Methodist Church's estimated £6 per week, both inclusive of tax rebates for covenants. The total sums involved seem huge, but it must be remembered that there are some 11,000 stipendiary clergy and lay workers and nearly 1.5 million members of church electoral rolls, apart from the thousands of other habitual attenders, well-wishers and occasional worshippers who are all potential donors. However, there are no fewer than 16,300 places of worship to maintain.

Contrary to what is generally believed, the State contributes no money to the Church of England (apart from some grants for historic buildings, in company with other denominations). It is the other way round. The Church has to contribute to the State in the form of VAT payable on repairs to the fabric of its church buildings.

17

The Discipline of the Church of England

Faith is more important than discipline. Nonetheless the Church of England, as an institution, has to have its disciplinary procedures, and because it is sometimes accused of not having any, it is necessary, for the sake of completeness, to explain what they are.

The Church of England has a somewhat different system of discipline from some other churches, relying for the most part on the self-discipline of its members, and regarding them as adults who must learn here on earth to discipline themselves in preparation for their future life in heaven.

DISCIPLINE OF LAY PEOPLE

While all parishioners are free to attend services in their parish church, no lay persons should receive the Holy Communion unless they have been confirmed, or are ready and desirous to be so. Permission may be given by the bishop in certain cases for specified unconfirmed young persons to receive the sacrament if their priest assures him that they are being instructed in the Christian faith, and intend to be confirmed when they reach the requisite age.

According to the Book of Common Prayer, a person who is an 'open and notorious evil liver' or those who have done serious wrong to a neighbour to the scandal of the congregation, shall be warned by the priest that they may not receive the sacrament until they have openly repented of what they have done. The same warning shall be given to two people who are behaving maliciously towards each other. This is rarely done.

MARRIAGE DISCIPLINE

If two people want to get married in church and one of them has a former partner still living, they should approach the parish priest of either of the parishes in which they live, and ask the vicar whether or not he or she is prepared to officiate at their wedding. The vicar, if unwilling to do so, may allow the parish church to be used by another priest who agrees to officiate at the wedding.

The reason for this somewhat odd situation is that there is some ambiguity in the present marriage discipline of the Church of England. Divorced and remarried persons are no longer debarred from receiving Holy Communion in the Church of England. Under State law, the Matrimonial Causes Act 1937 specifically allows remarriages in a Church of England church, but in 1957 Acts passed by the Convocations of Canterbury and York declared that clergy should not exercise this lawful liberty. (An Act of Convocation has more authority than a mere resolution, but the veto has no legal force.) There is no mention of the Convocations' veto in the canon law of the Church of England, as canon law does have legal force, and must therefore not be in conflict with the secular law of the land. However in 1981, when General Synod last debated the matter, it was agreed (by a majority of 72 per cent) that there are occasions when it would be proper for such a wedding to be celebrated in the parish church.

Unfortunately General Synod was unable to agree on the circumstances in which such a wedding in church would be justified. Some clergy still feel bound by the 1937 Act of Convocation and reject any idea of remarriage in church. Others feel that its authority has been fatally eroded by the Synod motion of 1981, and they therefore use their own discretion in allowing church weddings.

DISCIPLINE CONCERNING CHURCH BUILDINGS

A congregation may not make alterations in a parish church without permission. No permanent change can be made in the furnishings or structure of a parish church without obtaining from the chancellor of the diocese (its chief legal officer) a 'faculty' enabling this to happen.

DISCIPLINE CONCERNING SERVICES IN CHURCH

Before clergy or Lay Readers are authorised to take services in a parish church, a solemn declaration has to be taken to the effect that only the Book of Common Prayer will be used 'and none other save that is authorised by lawful authority'. The Parochial Church Council must approve before clergy may use services in the parish church from the Alternative Service Book.

DISCIPLINE CONCERNING CLERGY

Clergy are expected to exercise suitable self-discipline in their lives, and no bishop seeks to peer through the keyhole of the vicarage bedroom. What happens there is a matter for which a priest is accountable to God. But occasions do arise when action has to be taken to discipline a priest. The

Church of England has a complex system of church courts which exercise jurisdiction over breaches of clergy discipline. Under the Ecclesiastical Jurisdiction Measure clergy may be tried for serious, persistent or continuous neglect of duty, or for 'conduct unbecoming the office and work of a clerk in Holy Orders'. The latter includes drunkenness and sexual offences (but not divorce by irretrievable breakdown when no adultery by the priest is proven). Open cohabitation with a partner by gay clergy is regarded as inadmissible, according to a discussion paper issued by the house of bishops. Censures for breaches of discipline range from an official rebuke, temporary suspension from certain duties, and inhibition (disqualification for a time from performing any clerical functions) to deprivation (removal from a clerical post). Imprisonment by a secular court automatically effects deprivation. To this may be added deposition, that is to say, permanent removal from holy orders (although the ceremony of 'unfrocking a priest' is not now used). Bishops and archbishops may also be tried and censured. There is a complex system of appeals to higher courts. Legal action can prove very expensive. In a recent case, where a retrial had to be ordered, the total cost of the trials, including legal aid, amounted to some £350,000, and General Synod had to pass a supplementary budget in order to meet these costs.

A bishop may deal with a case summarily when a priest is willing, and when he admits his guilt. This prevents the unwelcome publicity of the Consistory Court, and it is this procedure that is usually followed. The archbishops keep lists of those censured. They are informed of the nature of their censure

and have confidential counsellors appointed to help
them if they so wish. Very rarely indeed does it happen that a bishop misbehaves, but in this case the
archbishop secures his resignation and he is no
longer licensed to officiate. With 10,000 clergy,
there are always a few cases of clergy discipline, but
these represent a very small proportion of the total
number of clergy. Not all cases involve ecclesiastical
law, for a bishop often deals pastorally with a situation to ensure that matters are put right and that the
offence is not repeated.

GENERAL

A copy of the canon law of the Church of England is
supposed to be kept in the vestry of a parish church,
to help in the observance of its rules and regula-
tions. Unlike some other churches, the Church of
England is not a legalistic church, although because
it is an established church it has a cumbrous and
expensive legal system. People are expected to exercise proper self-discipline in their lives, and the law
is usually invoked only when a public scandal devel-
ops. The Church of England prefers pastoral oversight to legal prosecution. Dioceses have a large
pastoral network, ranging from the rural dean
upwards, and most dioceses have counsellors whom
clergy may approach confidentially to help them in
difficult personal situations.

18

The Church of England and the Anglican Communion

A national church which stands on its own is likely to be deficient in many ways. It will probably be isolated from movements of thought and practice in other churches. It is likely to be parochial in outlook, reflecting national tendencies and prejudices. It will only with difficulty persuade its members that they are part of the one, holy, catholic and apostolic Church dispersed throughout the world.

The Church of England, when it was first reformed, did stand alone. But it no longer does. It is part of the worldwide Anglican Communion. This came about unintentionally and Anglicans see in this the providence of God, which has resulted in some 70 million Anglicans worldwide, with 64,000 independent congregations, dispersed in some 450 dioceses all over the world in a total of 164 countries.

THE FIRST STAGE

The Anglican Communion began with the spread of the British Empire, and with Britons migrating to countries such as America and Canada. Originally churches overseas were part of the Church of England and were regarded as extensions of the Diocese of London. The United States was the first country to have its own bishop when it achieved political independence from Britain. There followed the formation of dioceses in Canada, and then India, Australia, New Zealand and South Africa.

MISSIONARY SOCIETIES

A new stage began with the work of missionary
societies. Christians felt the impulse to convert the
heathen and to save them from hell, and founded
hospitals, schools and colleges as well as churches.
The first missionary society was SPCK, the publishers
of this book. The Society for the Propagation of the
Gospel (SPG) was founded back in 1701, to help
existing churches; in 1968 it joined with the
Universities' Mission to Central Africa, founded in
1857 in response to Livingstone's call for the con-
version of Africa, and became the present United
Society for the Propagation of the Gospel (USPG).
The South American Missionary Society (SAMS)
began in 1844. Many devoted men and women went
– and continue to go – overseas to give themselves to
spreading the good news of Christ, and building up
Christian communities overseas. Gradually these
churches produced their own clergy and leaders,
and missionaries are now needed to support rather
than to organise these churches.

INDEPENDENCE

These churches thrived, and new church congregations were formed far beyond the bounds of the
Empire. After World War II, most of these churches
became independent, usually in advance of political
independence. The dioceses were no longer under
the jurisdiction of the Archbishop of Canterbury,
but were part of independent provinces. There are
now 31 autonomous churches; some of them are
provinces, while others, like the Church of England
or the Protestant Episcopal Church of the United
States, are groups of provinces formed into a single

church. For those regions where the numbers of Anglicans are too small to sustain an independent province, regional councils have been developed. These independent provinces are self-supporting. Most dioceses in England and the United States have a partner diocese in the Third World, but a very small proportion of the funds of the poorer churches comes from their partners. Membership has tended to decline in the Mother Church and in the 'old commonwealth', but in the Third World membership is growing, and the growth is estimated at 3,000 new members per day. Eighteen of the 31 member churches of the Anglican Communion are in the Third World.

The Church of England, with its provinces of Canterbury and York, is the only church established by law in the Anglican Communion. Members of the other churches in the Communion often feel that members of the Church of England have little idea of what it means to be simply one church among others, without any particular form of recognition.

The Anglican Communion is much smaller than the Roman Catholic and the Orthodox Churches, and it is not so large as, say, the worldwide Methodist and Baptist Churches. Nonetheless it can probably lay claim to being the most widespread communion after the Roman Catholic Church.

MEMBERSHIP OF THE ANGLICAN COMMUNION
The Anglican Communion's distinguishing mark is that its churches are in communion with the Archbishop of Canterbury, who holds a position of honour in the Anglican Communion, but no jurisdiction over provinces other than his own. The

member churches are linked to one another by ties of affection and common loyalty, not by church law. There is also a common ethos, and while autonomous churches have their own prayer books, they have a common ancestry in the Book of Common Prayer. Some churches still refer to the Thirty-Nine Articles of Religion (see page 21) which used to be the common standard of doctrine throughout the communion; but this is no longer the case in England and most other Anglican churches.

DECENTRALISATION AND CO-ORDINATION

The history of the Anglican Communion, in contrast, say, to the Roman Catholic Church, has been one of increasing decentralisation. What began as an offshoot of the diocese of London has now emerged as a communion of autonomous churches. It is not easy for all these churches to keep in step with one another. For example, some of them ordain women to the priesthood and some do not. Every ten years the Archbishop of Canterbury invites the bishops of the Anglican Communion to meet with him in conference at Lambeth, and although the conference resolutions do not in themselves have any binding force on the autonomous churches of the Communion, they have great authority. The long interval between these conferences has resulted in the need for more frequent contacts in our present fast moving world. The Archbishop of Canterbury is President of the Primates' Committee of these different churches; there is also the Anglican Consultative Council (ACC), consisting of representative bishops, priests and lay people, which co-ordinates activities and ensures proper intercommunication on important matters. There is an Executive Officer of the ACC with a small staff.

ECUMENICAL ACTIVITIES

Some parts of the Anglican Communion have left to form part of a united church (for example, the Church of South India and the Church of North India), and their representatives are now invited to the Lambeth Conferences. Anglicans in China have taken a leading part in the formation of the united Chinese Protestant Church. There have been international dialogues between the Anglican Communion and other worldwide churches – not only the Roman Catholic Church, but also the Lutheran World Federation, the Orthodox Churches, and the World Alliance of Reformed Churches. It has also consulted with other churches through the Faith and Order Department of the World Council of Churches.

SUMMARY

As we have seen, it was not the intention of the Church of England to start a new communion. But it happened, and the result is that the Anglican Communion is distinctive among the worldwide Christian communions. It is decentralised, in as much as there is no central authority. Its cohesion comes from its common ancestry, and from the ties of Christian affection and common loyalty which have been engendered. At the same time it is an episcopal communion with bishops and archbishops, with primacy of respect given to the Archbishop of Canterbury who functions as an unofficial patriarch, without any jurisdictional or doctrinal powers. Each Archbishop of Canterbury tries to visit the other churches during his period of office, in addition to his remaining diocesan duties in Canterbury and his work as Primate of All England, and this adds greatly to his burdens.

19

The Church of England and the Ecumenical Movement

The Church of England has in the past played a key part in the movement to bring together the splintered churches of Christendom so that they are structurally as well as spiritually the one, holy, catholic and apostolic church. Attempts have been made to reunite churches both in the United Kingdom and worldwide.

EARLY MOVES

The Elizabethan Settlement, aimed at producing a national church for all English people, did not succeed in its aim. At the Restoration, King Charles II in 1660 summoned a conference at Worcester House in London, in an attempt to get the Presbyterians back into the Church of England under a modified system of episcopacy. It nearly succeeded, and it seems that its failure was due to the triumphalism of Anglicans restored to power and to the King's desire to act by royal prerogative rather than through Parliament.

In 1717 and 1718 Archbishop Wake held a correspondence with leaders of the Gallican Church (the Roman Catholic Church in France) which resented papal interference in its affairs. This came to nothing with the death of the chief French correspondent. Around the same time Archbishop Wake also recognised the Moravian Church as truly episcopal. In 1719 he said that he would welcome a closer union with all the Reformed bodies 'at almost any price'. Later he also initiated dialogue with the patriarchs of the Orthodox Churches. Although none of these moves bore any fruit, they do show early attempts at reunion.

RELATIONS WITH PROTESTANTS OUTSIDE BRITAIN

In 1841 there was a plan for a Protestant bishop in Jerusalem, to be nominated alternately by the Church of England and the Prussian Lutheran Church, but it lapsed because of the outcry among high churchmen in England.

Towards the end of the nineteenth century discussions began with the Scandinavian Lutheran churches which led to full communion with those churches which had retained the apostolic succession at the Reformation. The Poovoo Declaration of 1994 proposed that full communion be extended to all the Nordic and Scandinavian Lutheran churches. Recently intercommunion (a more limited agreement enabling members to receive the Holy Communion in each other's churches) has been established between the Church of England and Lutheran churches generally.

RELATIONS WITH THE ORTHODOX AND OLD CATHOLICS

Official relations between the Church of England and the Orthodox Churches (which split from Rome in the eleventh century) began as far back as 1841. In many ways Anglicanism has affinities with the Orthodox, especially in refusing to define mysteries too precisely. Friendships have ripened, and some Orthodox Churches actually recognised Anglican orders. In this century an Anglican–Orthodox joint commission was set up, but the ordination of women to the priesthood, to which the Orthodox are resolutely opposed, has cooled relationships somewhat.

The Old Catholics centred in Holland, Germany and Switzerland, who began their breach with Rome in 1724 and were later joined by others who rejected the Roman decree of papal infallibility and the Pope's claim to universal jurisdiction, declared themselves in full communion with the Church of England in 1932.

RELATIONS WITH THE ROMAN CATHOLIC CHURCH

In 1890 Viscount Halifax struck up a friendship with the Abbé Portal of Paris, which led to conversations about the validity of Anglican orders. Both the Archbishop of Canterbury and the Pope were kept informed and expressed friendly interest. The latter set up an enquiry into Anglican orders, which led to the publication of the bull *Apostolicae Curae*, pronouncing them 'absolutely null and utterly void' (see appendix).

A new start was made at the Lambeth Conference of 1920, when an 'Appeal to all Christian People' was issued, based on the 'Lambeth Quadrilateral' of Holy Scripture, the Apostles' Creed, the two sacraments of baptism and the Eucharist, and the historic episcopate. Halifax and Portal began 'Conversations' on unity between 1921 and 1923 at Malines. Their importance was that they envisaged reunion rather than the absorption of the Church of

England into the Roman Catholic Church. Rome brought these talks to an end with the death of Cardinal Mercier, under whose auspices they had been held.

A new initiative began with the visit of Archbishop Geoffrey Fisher to Rome in 1960, followed by the visit of Archbishop Michael Ramsey in 1966. This led to the setting up of the Anglican Roman Catholic International Commission, which issued a series of reports showing a very remarkable convergence between the two communions, on the subjects of the Eucharist, holy orders and authority. A new Commission has subsequently reported on salvation and on ethics. In 1982 Pope John Paul II visited Canterbury Cathedral during his visit to England, and issued a joint declaration with the Archbishop of Canterbury. However, the ordination of women to the priesthood has prevented further progress.

RELATIONS WITH THE FREE CHURCHES IN BRITAIN

A new initiative was taken by Geoffrey Fisher when he was Archbishop of Canterbury suggesting that the Free Churches in Britain should take 'episcopacy into their system'. This led in time to the Anglican Methodist Scheme of Reunion, under which the Methodists would first ordain bishops in stage 1 of the scheme, and would enjoy intercommunion with the Church of England, and then later in stage 2 both would merge into a single church. The Methodist Church ratified this scheme, but the Church of England could not quite find the three-quarters majority necessary for final ratification by General Synod, and it lapsed in 1972. The Methodist

Church in Britain has in 1994 asked for talks to be revived.

A further scheme involving the United Reformed Church also was later hatched under 'Covenanting for Unity' in 1980, but that too failed in General Synod.

However, the Church of England has authorised 'areas of ecumenical experiment' where members of different churches join in membership of a single congregation, with celebrations of Holy Communion both by Anglican priests and Free Church ministers. These churches feel somewhat exposed ecumenically, in as much as they practice an ecumenism which is far ahead of the other churches in the country.

COUNCILS OF CHURCHES

The Church of England featured prominently in the setting up of the World Council of Churches, first suggested by Archbishop William Temple in 1935. He, Dr J. H. Oldham and Bishop George Bell of Chichester took a leading part up to its foundation in 1948. Since that time the Church of England has been less active in its organisation. The British Council of Churches (of which the Roman Catholic Church was not a member) was closed down in 1992, and 'Churches Together in Britain' (of which the Roman Catholic Church is a member) has taken its place. It seeks to act not on its own, but through the churches of which it is composed. It appears very low key.

SUMMARY

In the past the Church of England has had a very

honourable history in ecumenical matters, prompted in part by its own pluralist composition. If such varied people can live together in one church, why cannot churches with different viewpoints also join together? However, more recently, ecumenical initiatives involving the Church of England have all foundered, since in the more immediate past it has been almost impossible to get the necessary three-quarters majority needed for any major change. (General Synod decided on this majority, instead of the normal two-thirds, for the Anglican Methodist scheme.) Traditionally the Church of England has had closer relations with the Free Churches than with the Church of Rome. It is only since the formation of ARCIC that that has changed; but the present situation suggests a further swing of the pendulum, exemplified by the Methodist Church's approach for renewed talks.

It may be doubted, however, whether organic reunion, which has been the object of the ecumenical movement this century, is an achievable goal. Some kind of mutual recognition of orders may be achieved which permits intercommunion; and there is also a greater determination on the part of the churches to work together in social policies as much as possible, and to do together all that does not have to be done apart.

20

Some Criticisms

A great deal of criticism has been levelled at the Church of England in the recent past, most of which is quite unjustified. For example, here are some remarks taken from a recent symposium *(Come On In: It's Awful)* directed against the Church of England: 'The faith and moral authority continue to disintegrate.' 'The C of E has lost its sense of direction: it doesn't know what it's for.' 'Its traditional *via media* has degenerated from an intellectual position to mere weakness of mind. Its public moral stances seem indistinguishable from those of a reasonably decent mildly Left-wing agnostic. Its retreat into self-government and its attack on the parish system make it less national and more sectarian. The clergy appear to know less and less. Churches were being closed, liturgies vandalised.' '. . . A general feeling among ordinary lay people that the C of E has betrayed them, through politicisation, liberalism and moral compromise.' 'In many people's opinion the ship is sinking while still at anchor.' The earlier chapters of this book have shown how grotesquely unfair and uninformed this kind of wild accusation is; and it is very hurtful to loyal Anglicans who believe in their church.

The complaints seem to be mostly about change of any kind; some of the targets are the newly authorised liturgies, new explorations of doctrine, the use of inclusive language, and the ethical priorities and socio-political pronouncements by church leaders. It must be said, however, that the same kind of complaints are made by some people against any attempt at *aggiornamento* (renewal) in the Roman Catholic Church. Criticisms come from those conservatives who think that the church, like Canute, can command the waves of change, and that it should refuse to inculturate itself into the rapidly changing society of England at the end of the twentieth century.

There are also criticisms about the Church of England's moderate stance on homosexuality and abortion from those with strong views on one side or the other, while the Church has to proceed with a real division of opinion in the ranks of its bishops, clergy and laity. We have already looked at these issues in chapter 14 on the moral teaching of the Church of England.

There are two further criticisms which still need to be mentioned.

FEMINISM

The Church of England is sometimes accused of bowing to feminism, although there are some who think that the Church still bears too many marks of male domination. We have already examined the theological reasons for ordaining women to the priesthood. Minor changes to liturgy, to avoid using 'man' or 'men' to include both men and women are now often made, and these conform with a change of usage in our society as a whole. The old usage can grate on those women who have been conscientised in such a way that they feel marginalised by the older usage. It should surely be a Christian concern that the language we use does not give offence to our fellow Christians. The word for God remains masculine (although of course God himself is without gender) for the same reason.

It remains to be seen how quickly outstanding women priests will be appointed to senior posts, and whether they will achieve a new style of more collaborative ministry.

RACISM

The Church of England on occasion has been outspoken against racism because it is one of the great evils of our time. Now that in the large cities of England there is a sizeable black population, the Church needs to make it even more clear that to discriminate against people on grounds of colour is contrary to Christian teaching, just as it is to discriminate on grounds of gender, class or race. It is particularly important for the Church to practice what it preaches about racism because in some large cities, ethnic minorities comprise a considerable proportion of church members (for example, in Birmingham, they represent 10 per cent of Anglican church membership). Criticism against the Church of England on the grounds that it is pro-Black is profoundly unChristian. If anything, there should be criticism over whether it is as yet sufficiently pro-Black.

GENERAL

Some criticisms of the Church of England are doubtless justified. We could all do better. No church is perfect. In the history of Christianity appalling sins have been committed not just by individual church members but also by whole churches. In this matter the Church of England is no better (and no worse) than other mainstream churches. To single it out for abuse in the way that has happened lately suggests some hidden agenda or antipathy on the part of those who do so. In an age of sweeping change which has included a degree of marginalisaton of religious institutions, a conservative backlash is inevitable. So too are calls for stronger leadership and a greater concentration on 'basics'. Pronouncements of a traditional kind are ignored by the mass media, but they give massive publicity to attacks on the church, and the public is undoubtedly influenced by this. But Jesus said: 'How blessed you are, when you suffer insults and persecution and every kind of calumny for my sake' (Matthew 5.13).

A PERSONAL VIEWPOINT

I have to confess that I am proud to be a member of the Church of England. It has many faults both of omission and of commission, and I am from time to time enraged by it. *Odi et amo* – I loathe it and I love it. I loathe its reluctance to change, its ecclesiastical parties, its occasional abuses. But I love its reformed Catholicism, its evangelical stance, its respect for truth, its comprehensiveness, its rich and varied spirituality, the informal dignity of its worship, its doctrinal stance, its social consciousness. Much as I admire other denominations, I could not belong to any other church.

21

The Future of the Church of England (with Some Statistics)

The future of the Church of England is in God's hands; but because God works through people to achieve his ends, our faithlessness may hinder his purposes. His Holy Spirit guides the whole church of God, but history shows that particular communions may rise or fall. This situation is inevitable when the one, holy, catholic and apostolic church is in schism, a tragic situation to which the multitude of different churches bears witness. Cultural differences also affect all the churches. For example, in Africa and the East churches are expanding rapidly. In Europe the mainstream churches are generally contracting in a very secular atmosphere, while sects are increasing. In Germany the membership of Protestant churches fell by 420,000 in 1993. (Figures for the Roman Catholic Church there are not to hand.) The Church of England is not immune from these general tendencies, although it is not as badly affected as some churches. Marc Europe (now known as Christian Research Ltd) is the only body which has attempted to assess churchgoing in England in all churches by means of a voluntary census. While its figures do not carry the same authority as the official census of churchgoing carried out in 1891 and 1901, they are the only statistics we have of all the churches in the land. According to the Marc Europe's report *Christian England*, published in 1991, the position of the Church of England is comparatively static, while the churches that have suffered the greatest losses in Britain are the Roman Catholic Church and the United Reformed Church; but since the statistics on which this judgment was based come from a voluntary census, they cannot be regarded as definitive.

ANGLICAN STATISTICS

Figures for baptisms, confirmations and average Sunday attendance, which registered a steep decline in the 1980s, have now become more stable. While there is growth, even large growth in some areas, in general there is a slight annual decline. Marc Europe's researches established that the main reason for this is the average age of church members. Younger people are not making up the numbers as older members die. A Mori poll in 1994 of 1,200 persons aged 15–35 found that a majority even of church members among them did not think that the church had much to offer them.

The peak in the average number of Sunday communicants in the early 1970s was due to the spread of the Parish Communion movement, displacing attendance at Morning and Evening Prayer. The number of baptisms may have been affected by the rigorist policies now adopted by some clergy, on the questionable grounds that, as children are most influenced by their parents, it is wrong to baptise infants unless the parents are regular churchgoers or promise to become such (see page 22). Whereas earlier it was customary for a young person to be confirmed, this is no longer the case; and so confirmands may be expected to be more serious in their intentions now than before. Yet when all these factors have been discounted, it still remains true that there is a small annual decline.

COMPARISON OF CHURCH OF ENGLAND AND ROMAN CATHOLIC STATISTICS

Current statistics quickly become out of date. Nonetheless it is of interest to compare statistics of different churches, although such comparison is not always easy. Roman Catholic numbers represent both England and Wales, and so figures for the Church in Wales have to be added to those of the Church of England to make a proper comparison. In some cases the figures for the Church in Wales and the Roman Catholic figures apply to 1993, whereas the latest figures available for the Church of England were mostly for 1992. The differences from year to year are not great.

Infant baptisms

Roman Catholic under 11	78,316
C of E 180,000	
+ Church in Wales 10,516	190,516

Usual Sunday attendance

Roman Catholic Mass attendance	1,277,617
Communicants: C of E 1,137,000	
+ Wales 47,650	1,184,650

Ordinations to the priesthood

Roman Catholic	53
C of E 348 + Wales 31	379

Number of serving priests

RC 4,128 diocesan + 1,888 religious	6,016
C of E (incl. non-diocesan) 12,343	
+ Wales 790	13,132

Church buildings open for worship

Roman Catholic	3,898
C of E 16,300	
+ Wales 1,560	17,860

THE FUTURE

We have already noted that Christianity tends to be
static or in decline in Europe, but that it is gaining
ground in Africa and the Americas. So far as the
Church of England is concerned, a diminishing
number of contributors will eventually find it harder
to support the present network of parishes, clergy
and parish churches of an established church. In
1993 for the first time some dioceses, with the present standards of weekly giving, found themselves
financially unable to take up all their allocation of
deacons. However, the average weekly giving in the
Church of England, compared with that of members
of the Methodist Church (see chapter 16) suggests
that there is plenty of room for considerably more
giving. Renewal movements are springing up. There
is no cause here for pessimism.

More important is the question of whether there is
any spiritual decline in our increasingly secular culture. This is a matter which affects all the churches,
not only the Church of England. At the moment the
faith is often expressed in ways that seem meaning-
less and irrelevant to those outside the Church.
Unless and until it can be satisfactorily inculturated
into our contemporary English society, in words and
images and concepts which make sense, some further overall decline seems inevitable. It is particularly important that the faith should be able to be
expressed convincingly within the subculture of

young people. Although morale is not as high in some regions as in others, there is little sign of spiritual decline within the Church of England; rather the contrary: morale is often higher than in the past.

The situation however calls for strong leadership. Vision, imagination and insight are needed to make the Christian faith seem attractive, credible and relevant to large numbers of unchurched people in our present secular culture. It is important to explain and commend Christianity in a situation where there is a spiritual vacuum, rather than continually to confront people with a spiritual challenge. Evangelical zeal is required, but it must be tempered with an appeal to reason.

However there is no cause for pessimism. There could well be a lasting spiritual renewal such as has happened before in these islands through the Evangelical Revival and the Oxford Movement. The future here is in God's hands, and depends on his Holy Spirit renewing his Church.

The Church of England has never seen itself as an end in itself. Comprised as it is of catholics, evangelicals and liberals, it has some unique contributions to make to the church of the future (as it is hoped this book makes clear). But it is an interim body, a sign for the future. It will, we hope, continue to exist in this country until the wounds which have broken apart the body of Christ have been healed; and by the time that happens, creeping disestablishment (if not reunion with other churches) is likely to have seen the breaking of legal ties with the State. Just as in India the Anglican Church has merged with other churches to form the Churches of North India and South India, so in this country a similar movement may eventually arise. If so, the Church of England will have served its time. On the other hand, increasing secularisation may force the church for a time into a non-institutional phase. Already there are signs of Christian believing without Christian belonging.

We simply do not know the future. Christians who have faith should also have hope. Whatever happens, the future is with God, and he can 'turn even the wrath of man to his praise'. For them that love God, all things work together for good.

Appendix: Roman Catholic Objections to Anglican Orders

CATHOLIC OBJECTIONS TO ANGLICAN ORDERS

Anglican orders have been recognised as valid by some Orthodox Churches. In the Roman Catholic Church, however, they are still officially regarded as 'absolutely null and utterly void', although not all Roman Catholics believe this. What follows is put in an appendix because it may appear a little too technical for some readers, but since the objection to Anglican orders by that Church is long standing and deep seated, I shall show that their arguments were ill founded.

It used to be held against the validity of Anglican orders that its priests were not invested with chalice and paten at their ordination; but this objection was dropped when it was pointed out that this did not happen in the early church, so that all subsequent ordinations, Roman or otherwise, would have to be regarded as null and void on these grounds. For this and other reasons there was pressure in the Roman Catholic Church to reconsider the matter, and this Pope Leo XIII duly did.

APOSTOLICAE CURAE

In 1896 Pope Leo XIII issued the encyclical *Apostolicae Curae* in which the negative judgment on Anglican orders was reinforced. Its chief arguments may be summarised as follows:

☐ It was asserted that the controversy had been definitively settled by Rome way back in the days of Edward VI.

☐ In the Church of England's new ordinal at the Reformation, the words used at the moment of ordination were simply 'Receive the Holy Ghost'. This did not in itself necessarily imply priesthood. The 'form' of ordination was therefore insufficient. It was a century later before there was added the phrase 'for the Office and Work of a Priest in the Church of God'; but by that time those carrying out ordinations had all been themselves ordained under the shorter phrase, and they therefore lacked power to carry out valid ordinations.

☐ The Pope affirmed that Anglican orders are defective not only in 'form' but also in 'intention'. The rejection of the Roman Catholic rite and introduction of a new rite without specific mention of a sacrificial priesthood and so on shows an intention contrary to that of the Roman Catholic Church. Nor could any subsequent bishop put things right, as he himself would have been consecrated by an invalid rite.

THE ARCHBISHOPS' RESPONSE

The then Archbishops of Canterbury and York made a weighty and powerful response to the Pope's encyclical. Their chief arguments may be summarised as follows:

☐ Any argument about deficiencies of Anglican form has equally to reckon with the difficulties in the Roman Catholic pontifical of those days, in which it was uncertain at what actual moment a priest was ordained, and in which the word 'bishop' was not mentioned during the prayers and benedictions of his consecration.

☐ So far as the practice of the Roman Court during the sixteenth century is concerned, there was much inconsistency and unevenness. As the Archbishops put it in their response:

> While many Edwardian Priests are found to have been deprived for various reasons, and particularly on account of entering into wedlock, none are so found, so far as we know, on account of defect of Order. Some received anointing as a supplement to their previous ordination . . . . Some, and perhaps the majority, remained in their benefices without reordination, nay were promoted in some cases to new cures.

☐ The Church need not and should not insist on a fixed form of ordination, but simply words appropriate to what is being done, as is the case with other sacraments. For while the laying on of hands is agreed to be the form of the sacrament of confirmation, the Orthodox Church regards chrism (consecrated oil) as the form, and in the past in the Roman Church it has been conferred on occasion simply by stretching of the hands in the direction of those to be confirmed. Precedent therefore suggests differences of form.

☐ As for the papal insistence on the insufficiency of the phrase 'Receive the Holy Ghost' at an ordination, the phrase occurs, without further addition, in the Roman pontifical current at the time at the consecration of a bishop. In both Roman and Anglican ordinals the function of the office is explained in other parts of the rite. The addition of the words 'for the Office and Work of a Priest (or Bishop)' added to the Anglican ordinal in 1662 was aimed at clarifying the rite not for Roman Catholics but for Presbyterians.

❐ It is certainly the intention of the Anglican Communion service that sacrifice should be offered: we continue a perpetual memory of the precious death of Christ; we offer the sacrifice of praise and thanksgiving; we represent before the Father the sacrifice of the cross; we offer the sacrifice of ourselves to God. (A similar breadth of meaning to sacrifice is to be found in the Roman Mass of that period.) To demand that an ordinal should contain explicitly the conferral of the power on a priest to offer sacrifice would actually invalidate the most ancient Roman ordination services, as would the insistence on the giving of authority to forgive sins. Similarly, to insist on the use of 'high priest' in the service to describe the office of a bishop would be contrary to ancient precedents.

VALIDITY OF ANGLICAN ORDERS

These arguments and counterarguments are inevitably somewhat technical. Nonetheless it is hard to deny that the arguments of *Apostolicae Curae* were definitively refuted by the archbishops. What is more, Vatican archives, opened up to the year 1903, have since shown that the expert theologians advising the Pope did not agree. Despite agreed statements on the Eucharist and on Ministry and

Ordination by ARCIC, and a request that the matter be further reconsidered, *Apostolicae Curae* has not been withdrawn, so that the official Roman Catholic view remains, alas, unchanged.

Suggestions for Further Reading

General
> G. Davie, *Religion in Britain since 1945* (Darton, Longman and Todd, 1944).

1. *The Church of England up to the Reformation*
> Owen Chadwick, *The Reformation* (Pelican, 1964).
> J.R.H. Moorman, *A History of the Church of England* (Black, 1953).

2. *The Reformation Settlement*
> J.W.C. Wand, *History of the Modern Church* (Methuen,1953).
> J.R.H. Moorman, *A History of the Church of England.*
> E. Duffy, *The Stripping of the Altars* (Yale University Press, 1992).

3. *The Authority of the Church of England*
> H. Montefiore, *So Near and Yet So Far* (SPCK, 1986).
> C. Hill and E. Yarnold (eds), *The Search for Unity* (SPCK, 1994).
> *Towards a Church of England: Response to BEM and ARCIC* (C.I.O., 1985).
> G.R. Evans, *Authority in the Church* (Canterbury Press,1990).
> D.L. Edwards, *What is Catholicism?* (Mowbray, 1994).

4. *The Doctrine of the Church of England*
> Archbishops' Commission, *Doctrine in the Church*

of England (SPCK, 1957).

Doctrine Commission of the Church of England, *Christian Believing* (SPCK, 1976).

Doctrine Commission of the Church of England, *Believing in the Church* (SPCK, 1981).

House of Bishops, *The Nature of Christian Belief* (C.I.O., 1986).

5. *The Worship of the Church of England*
   C. Buchanan, B.T. Lloyd, H. Miller (eds), *Anglican Worship Today* (Collins, 1980).

   R.C.D. Jasper, *The Development of Anglican Liturgy 1662–1980* (SPCK, 1989).

6. *The Church of England by Law Established*
   Archbishops' Commission, *Church and State 1970* (C.I.O., 1970).

   Adrian Hastings, *Church and State: The English Experience* (University of Exeter, 1981).

   Peter Cornwell, *Church and Nation* (Blackwell, 1983).

   J. Habgood, *Church and Nation in a Secular Age* (Darton, Longman and Todd, 1983).

   Colin Buchanan, *Cut the Connection* (Darton, Longman and Todd, 1994).

7. *Spirituality in the Church of England*
   Two Anglican books on spirituality are:
   Evelyn Underhill, *Mysticism* (Methuen, 1923), and
   Kenneth Leech, *True God* (Sheldon, 1985).
   See also the current *Library of Anglican Classics* ed. Susan Howatch (Mowbray).

8. *Saints in the Church of England*
   Donald Attwater, *Penguin Dictionary of Saints*

(Penguin, 1978).
For Anglican post-Reformation saints, see:
S.L. Ollard *et al.* (eds), *Dictionary of English Church History* (Mowbray, 1948).

9. *Pluralism in the Church of England*
James Dunn, *Unity and Diversity in the New Testament* (SCM Press, 1977).
Christopher Evans in *Christian Believing*.

10. *The Validity of Anglican Orders: Deacons, Priests and Bishops*
Anglican Orders: The Bull of His Holiness Pope Leo XIII and the Answer of the Archbishops of England (SPCK, 1943).
Gregory Dix, *The Question of Anglican Orders* (Dacre 1956).
F. Clark, *Anglican Orders and Defect of Intention* (London, 1956).

11. *Anglicans and the Ordination of Women to the Priesthood*
M. Webster, *A New Strength, A New Song* (Mowbray, 1994).

12. *The Clergy of the Church of England*
Christian England (Marc Europe, 1991).
See statistics in *Church Statistics* (CHP, 1993).
Numbers in Ministry (ABM Publications, 1994).
Church of England Year Book (CHP, 1994).
Catholic Directory 1994.

13. *The Laity*
Kathleen Bliss, *We the People* (SCM Press, 1963).

14. *The Moral Teaching of the Church of England*
ARCIC, *Morals, Communion and the Church* (CTS/

SPCK, 1994).

15. *The Church of England and Education*
    Report of the Durham Commission, *The Fourth R*
    (SPCK, 1970).

16. *The Finances of the Church of England*
    Church Commissioners, Reports Commissioned
    by the Archbishop of Canterbury (1993).
    See annual reports of the Church
    Commissioners and the Central Board of
    Finance.
    Church Statistics (1993) and *The Church of England
    Handbook* (1994).

17. *The Discipline of the Church of England*
    Canon Law of the Church of England (CHP).
    Ecclesiastical Jurisdiction Measure in *Halsbury's
    Statutes of England (3rd edn): Ecclesiastical Law.*

18. *The Church of England and the Anglican
    Communion*
    See reports of the Lambeth Conferences
    published by SPCK.

19. *The Church of England and the Ecumenical
    Movement*
    Barry Till, *The Churches' Search for Christian Unity*
    (Pelican, 1972).
    David Paton, *Anglicans and Unity* (Mowbray,
    1962).

20. *Some Criticisms*
    Joanna Bogle (ed.), *Come On In: It's Awful*
    (Gracewing, 1994).

21. *The Future of the Church of England*
    D.L. Edwards, *The Future of Christianity* (Hodder

and Stoughton, 1993).

A. McGrath, *The Renewal of Anglicanism* (SPCK, 1993).

Books on Anglicanism

S. Sykes and J. Booty (eds), *The Study of Anglicanism* (SPCK, 1988).

S. Sykes, *Unashamed Anglicanism* (Darton, Longman and Todd, 1995).

Glossary of Church Terms

Here is a list of church terms, by no means exhaustive, but likely to be sufficient for most purposes

Abbot	Head of an abbey of *monks*
Acolyte	Lay assistant in church ceremonial, including attendance at the altar and candle-bearing
Advent	Beginning of the church's year, referring to the four weeks before Christmas
Aisle	Division in church building, or passage between row of pews
Altar	Table used for celebration of Holy Communion
Alternative Service Book	The new (1980) prayer book used as an alternative to the old one
Anglican Communion	Autonomous churches linked by communion with the Archbishop of Canterbury
Anthem	Sacred music and singing performed by a choir
Apostolic succession	Succession of bishops and clergy linked in the apostolic faith with the primitive church through the

	laying on of hands with prayer
Apportionment	Financial requirement on parishes by the *diocese* for clergy *stipends*, and diocesan and central administration
Archbishop	The leading *bishop* or *metropolitan* of a province with certain jurisdictional functions in the *province*
Archdeacon	Ecclesiastical dignitary next below a *bishop*, with particular responsibility for the maintenance of church buildings and discipline
Area Bishop	Suffragan bishop with enhanced powers over an area of a *diocese*
Augmentation	Money from the living church used to augment the endowment income of a parish to the level of the standard *stipend* agreed in a diocese
Bands	Two white tabs worn at collar level by clergy and lawyers
Banns	Notice of two persons intending matrimony to be read out in their parish churches for three consecutive Sundays beforehand, inviting people to make any legal objections
Baptism	Immersion of infant or adult in water (or pouring water over the

	head) in the name of the Trinity as Christian initiation
Benefice	An ecclesiastical post with *care of souls* in a parish and a parsonage house with right of *freehold* until retiring age
Bishop	The father-in-God of a *diocese* and its chief ecclesiastical officer
Bishop's Council	Partly elected, partly *ex officio* body to advise the *bishop* and to act on behalf of the Diocesan *Synod* if necessary
Book of Common Prayer	The church's prayer book, dating from 1662
Calendar	List of the church's annual seasons, festivals and commemorations
Canon	Member of a cathedral *chapter,* either honorary or residential (full-time)
Canon Law	The church's laws which form part of the law of the land
Cure	From the Latin *cura* (care), refers to a post carrying with it pastoral care
Cassock	Long close (usually black) tunic worn by clergy and lay assistants
Catechism	The church's teaching in question and answer form, used in

	the past for instructing children, and often learnt by heart
Catechist	Lay church worker in missionary areas of the church
Cathedral	'Mother church' of the *diocese*, where the *bishop* has his *cathedra* or seat
Catholic	The word means 'universal', but has come to mean one who adheres to the church's early traditions
Censer	Used for burning and swinging incense in church
Chalice	Cup used for Holy Communion
Chancel	That part of the church beyond the nave towards the east end
Chancellor	Either a *cathedral* dignitary, or the chief legal officer of a *diocese*
Chapter	The collegiate body, headed by *dean* or *provost*, in charge of a cathedral; also a body formed by the clergy of a rural deanery
Chapel of ease	A church in a *parish* additional to the parish church
Charge	Formal exhortation by a *bishop*
Chasuble	Outer garment worn by priest celebrating the Holy Communion

Chimere	Long outer garment (red or black) worn by *bishops*
Chrism	Consecrated oil for anointing
Church Commissioners	Body set up by Parliament to take charge of the church's endowments
Church schools	Schools with a Church of England foundation, which form part of the State system of education
Churches Together in England	Interdenominational body set up by the churches to foster working together
Churchwarden	Chief lay officer of a parish
Clerk in Holy Orders	Legal name for a clergyman
Confirmation	Laying on of hands with prayer by a bishop, completing Christian initiation
Confirmation of election	Legal ceremony whereby someone nominated to a bishopric is officially recognised
Consecration	Religious rite whereby a person is made a *bishop*
Convent	House occupied by a community of *nuns*
Consistory Court	Chief legal court of a *diocese*

Conventional district	Area of a *parish* which functions autonomously
Convocation	Body of elected clergy *(proctors)* in a *province*
Cope	Long and often ornate outer garment worn by bishops and clergy
Court of Arches	The highest ecclesiastical court of the Church of England
Creed	Summary of the church's faith, used in worship
Crosier	*Bishop's* pastoral staff
Crown Appointments Committee	Body of twelve people charged with recommending to the crown two names for a vacant diocesan bishopric
Crucifer	The bearer of the ceremonial cross in worship
Curate	Ordained assistant of a *vicar* or *rector*
Curtilege .	That part of the site of a parsonage house other than the actual building
Deacon	Junior ordained minister, usually for a year, unable as yet to pronounce the blessing or absolution, or to celebrate Holy Communion

Deaconess	Member of a female lay order, with duties the same as those of a *deacon*
Dean	Chief dignitary of a *cathedral*, who heads its *chapter*
Deanery	Official residence of a *dean*
Declaration of Assent	Statement of loyalty to the Church of England required of a *bishop, priest, deacon, deaconess, Reader* and some other lay officers
Defender of the Faith	Honorific title given by the Pope to Henry VIII, used by his successors
Diocese	The administrative and pastoral area where *parishes* are grouped together, and owe allegiance to the diocesan *bishop* concerned
Doctor of the Church	A person recognised by the Church as one of its seminal thinkers
Ecclesiastical Commission	Body set up by Parliament early in the nineteenth century to make a fairer distribution of the Church of England's assets, and to act as trustee
Ecclesiastical Committee	Committee drawn from both the House of Lords and the House of Commons to examine *Measures*

agreed by General *Synod* and to pronounce them 'expedient' or 'inexpedient', before Parliament votes on them

Ecumenical   The word is derived from the Greek, which means 'the whole inhabited world' and is used to refer to the collaboration and reunion of all Christendom

Encyclical   The word means 'circular', and refers to a formal pronounce-ment of the Pope circularised to the Roman Catholic Church

Enthronement   Ceremony in which a new diocesan *bishop* is received and welcomed in his *cathedral* church

Establishment   Used loosely to refer to the network of power and influence which determines government policies; when used of the Church of England it refers to its official status as established by law and recognised as the church of the land

Eucharist   Derived from the Greek 'thanksgiving', a word for Holy Communion

Evangelicals   Those Christians whose faith is primarily bible-based

Evangelist   One who spreads abroad the

good news of the gospel

Evensong	Evening Prayer according to the *Book of Common Prayer*
Exposition	Display of consecrated bread as an aid to worship
Faculty	A legal permit to make alterations in churches
Freehold	The right of the holder of a *benefice* to hold it undisturbed until retiring age providing no ecclesiastical offence has been committed
Free Churches	Those Protestant churches in England which are 'free' of the constraints of the established church
Fees	Sums due to clergy for carrying out certain ecclesiastical duties (especially weddings, funerals and cremations, but not *baptisms*)
Friar	A *religious* professed in the Society of St Francis
Glebe	Land belonging to the church which formerly formed part of the *benefice* of an *incumbent*, now administered centrally
Holy Communion	Liturgical celebration of the Lord's Supper

Homily	Sermon
Hood	Overgarment placed round the neck and hanging down the back which shows by shape and colour a person's degree and university
Incense	Burnt in catholic ceremonial, the smoke symbolising the ascent of prayer to God
Incumbent	The *priest* in charge of a *benefice*
Inhibition	Suspension of a *priest* from performing priestly functions
Institution	Ceremony by which a *bishop* authorises a *priest* to begin his *incumbency*
Intercommunion	Freedom to offer and receive Communion to and from another church denomination
Laity	Originally referring to the whole people of God, now used to describe members of the Church who are not ordained
Lambeth Conference	Decennial meeting of all *bishops* of the Anglican Communion, convoked by the Archbishop of Canterbury
Lectern	Reading desk for the public proclamation of Scripture
Lectionary	Prescribes which portions of

	Scripture shall be read during liturgical services
Letters Patent	Authorisation by the Crown (for example, for the consecration of a *bishop*)
Licence	Authorisation for a *priest* or *Reader* to minister within a *diocese*
Liturgy	Originally referring to the order of Holy Communion, now refers to all formal services
Liturgical colour	Different colours denote different seasons or occasions in the church's year; green for normal, red for Pentecost or for martyrs, white for Christmas, Easter and saints' days, purple for penitential seasons, and black (or white) for funerals and requiems
Local Ecumenical Project	Areas where worshippers are joint members of the collaborating churches, and served by ministers of these denominations
Mass	Derived from 'Ite missa est' at the end of the rite, the Latin-based word for Holy Communion
Martyr	One who gives his or her life for the Christian faith
Matins	Morning Service according to the *Book of Common Prayer*

Measure	Legal enactment agreed by General *Synod*
Metropolitan	*Archbishop* of a *province*
Ministry	Meaning service, the word describes the work of a lay person, *priest* or *bishop*
Missionary	One who spends his or her life spreading the gospel, at home or overseas
Mitre	Liturgical headgear worn by a *bishop* with chasuble or cope
Modernist	One who wishes to modernise the Church, often sitting light to traditional doctrine
Monk	Male *religious* vowed to chastity, poverty and obedience
Nave	Derived from the Latin word for ship, refers to the main part of a church building reserved for the *laity*
Non-conformist	One who does not conform to the Church of England as by law established
Nun	Female *religious* vowed to chastity, poverty and obedience
Orders	The state of being a *deacon*, *priest* or *bishop*

Ordinal	Services of ordination
Ordination	The rite by which people become *priests* or *deacons*
Parish	A legal area whose inhabitants have rights in its parish church
Parochial Church Council	Elected body in a *parish* to co-operate and to take counsel with the *priest* in charge, and to supervise the finances of the *parish* church
Paten	Small plate on which the bread of Holy Communion is consecrated
Patron	Person or body with the right to nominate (after consultation) a priest to an *incumbency* in a vacancy
Perpetual Curate	*Priest* in charge of a *conventional district*
Pix	Vessel for carrying the *Reserved Sacrament*
Priest	One who is ordained to assist the *bishop* by acting as his representative in a parish
Primate	Senior *bishop* or *archbishop* of an autonomous church of the *Anglican Communion*
Proctor	*Priest* elected to represent local clergy in *Convocation* and General *Synod*

Province	Grouping of *dioceses* under an *archbishop*
Provost	Chief officer of a cathedral *chapter* in more recent foundations
Queen Anne's Bounty	Fund given to the church by Queen Anne by her renunciation of annates, or the first year's emoluments of a *priest* taking up fresh office in the church
Quota	The share of the moneys required by a *diocese* calculated according to the resources of each parish
Reader	Lay person trained and licensed to preach and to take services other than celebrating at Holy Communion
Rector	The word means 'ruler' and was used to describe *incumbents* entitled to the rectorial or greater tithe; now an honorific title
Red Letter Day	Major feast day so designated in the church calendar
Reformation	Sixteenth-century movement across Europe which resulted in breakaways from the Roman Catholic Church
Registrar	Diocesan legal officer working

	under the *chancellor* and acting as legal adviser to the *bishop*
Requiem	Holy Communion celebrated at a funeral, or with special intention to pray for someone who has died
Religious	Clergy or laity who have taken vows to live in poverty, chastity and obedience within a religious order of *monks, nuns* or *friars*
Reserved Sacrament	Consecrated bread and wine retained or 'reserved' after a liturgical celebration, to be used for the sick not able to be present
Rochet	White overgarment not unlike a surplice worn with chimere by a *bishop*
Rosary	Beads used as an aid to prayer
Royal Peculiar	Church within the personal jurisdiction of the monarch
Rural Dean	*Priest* who is appointed by the *bishop* with certain duties, who presides over meetings of the local clergy *chapter* in a *deanery*
Sacristan	Person who looks after vestments, sacred vessels, and so on
Saint	Used to designate a person of special holiness, often marked

	out for commemoration in the church's calendar
Scarf	Long scarf-like garment worn with surplice and hood as part of 'choir dress'; those worn by clergy are black, while Readers' scarves are blue
Server	An assistant to the celebrant at Holy Communion
Sidesman or woman	One who assists in taking the collection and similar duties at church services
Stave	Ceremonial stick carried by *churchwarden* (originally to ward off any trouble-seekers)
Stipend	The regular income of the clergy
Stole	Coloured type of scarf, worn for celebrating sacraments
Suffragan bishop	A bishop who assists the diocesan *bishop*
Supreme Governor	Title assumed by Queen Elizabeth I, with functions now discharged under a constitutional monarchy through Parliament and the Prime Minister
Surplice	White garment worn over a cassock
Synod	A gathering of *bishops,* clergy

	and people to take counsel and make decisions
Theological college	Seminary for clergy
Thirty-Nine Articles	Statement of Anglican faith to which assent formerly had to be given by candidates for ordination
Thurible	Vessel for burning *incense*
Tithe	One-tenth of the produce of the land which had formerly to be given to the parish priest
Title	Initial appointment of a *deacon* on ordination
Uniate	A church which keeps its own liturgy and customs (for example married priests) but which is in communion with the Bishop of Rome
Verger	One who has the care of the church building, and who may escort church processions
Vestments	Clothes worn in church ceremonial for worship
Vicar	*Priest* in charge of a parish, who functions 'vicariously' for the *bishop*
Vicar Choral	*Priest* who leads the singing in a *cathedral*

Vicar General	*Priest* who acts in legalities in the absence of the *bishop*
Vigil	An all-night watch of prayer
Voluntary Aided School	School mostly paid for by the State, but with the majority of its governors appointed by the foundation
Voluntary Controlled School	School wholly paid for by the State, but with only a minority of its governors appointed by the foundation
Wafer	Used instead of bread in the Holy Communion
Wand	Ceremonial staff carried by a *verger*
World Council of Churches	A body with representatives of most churches worldwide, apart from the Roman Catholic Church